CYBER LAW
IN
INDIA

Simply In Depth

Information Technology Act, 2000
ITA-2000

Ajit Singh

Cyber Law In India Simply In Depth

For information about this title or to order other books and/or electronic media, contact the publisher:

Ajit Singh
ajit_singh24@yahoo.com
http://www.ajitvoice.in

ACKNOWLEDGEMENT

This piece of study of Cyber Law In India is an outcome of the encouragement, guidance, help and assistance provided to me by our colleagues, Sr. faculties, Tech-friends and our family members.

As an aknowledgement, I would like to take the opportunity to express my deep sense of gratitude to all those who played a crucial role in the successful completion of this book, especially to our sr. students.This book is resultant of several round of regular discussions held with many IT professionals (Ex-students) & Sr Advocates of India, over the years.

My primary goal here was to provide a sufficient introduction and details of the Cyber Law In India, so that the students can have an efficient knowledge about Cyber Crime & Law. It presupposes that knowledge of the principles and concepts of the Information Technology is required. On the same note, any errors and inaccuracies are my responsibility and suggestions in this regard are warmly welcomed!

I would like to thank our mentor and valued guardian, *Prof Dr. Bal Gangadhar Prasad* (HOD-Dept of Mathematics, Patna University) for setting a very high standard of writing about Cyber Crime & Law in India and for providing valuable suggestions in practical design of this book.

I hope that the readers will like this book and find it useful in learning the concepts and role of Cyber Law in India.

Thank You !!

Ajit Singh

PREFACE

Share the knowledge,
Strenghten the surrounding......!!!

The study/learning of Cyber Law in India is a part of computer science as well as law education courses across the several Universities of India. This textbook is intended as a guide for an explanatory course of Cyber Law In India for the Graduate and Post Graduate Students of several universities across the India.

To The Student

As we all know that this is the era where most of the things are done usually over the internet starting from online dealing to the online transaction. Since the web is considered as worldwide stage, anyone can access the resources of the internet from anywhere. The internet technology has been using by the few people for criminal activities like unauthorized access to other's network, scams etc. These criminal activities or the offense/crime related to the internet is termed as cyber crime. In order to stop or to punish the cyber criminals the term "Cyber Law" was introduced. We can define cyber law as it is the part of the legal systems that deals with the Internet, cyberspace, and with the legal issues. It covers a broad area, encompassing many subtopics as well as freedom of expressions, access to and utilization of the Internet, and online security or online privacy. Generically, it is alluded as the law of the web.

The principle target of my book is to spread the knowledge of the crimes or offences that take place through the internet or the cyberspace, along with the laws that are imposed against those crimes and criminals. I am additionally trying to focus on the safety in cyberspace.

Feedback

I have attempted to wash out every error in our first edition of this book after being reviewed by lots of scholars of Computer Science, but as happens with Computer typing – "A few bugs difficult to understand shall remain" – and therefore, suggestions from students that may lead to improvement of next edition in shortcoming future are highly appreciated.

*Conclusive suggestions and criticism always go a long way in enhancing any endeavour. I request all readers to email us their valuable comments / views / feedback for the betterment of the book at **ajit_singh24@yahoo.com** mentioning the title and author name in the subject line. Please report any piracy spotted by you as well . I* would be glad to hear suggestions from you.

I hope, you enjoy reading this book as much as I have enjoyed writing it. I would be glad to hear suggestions from you.

CONTENTS

1

INTRODUCTION

"Cyber" is a prefix used to describe a person, thing, or idea as part of the computer and information age. Taken from *kybernetes*, Greek word for "steersman" or "governor," it was first used in cybernetics, a word coined by Norbert Wiener and his colleagues. The virtual world of internet is known as cyberspace and the laws governing this area are known as Cyber laws and all the netizens of this space come under the ambit of these laws as it carries a kind of universal jurisdiction. Cyber law can also be described as that branch of law that deals with legal issues related to use of inter-networked information technology. In short, cyber law is the law governing computers and the internet.

The growth of Electronic Commerce has propelled the need for vibrant and effective regulatory mechanisms which would further strengthen the legal infrastructure, so crucial to the success of Electronic Commerce. All these regulatory mechanisms and legal infrastructures come within the domain of Cyber law.

Cyber law is important because it touches almost all aspects of transactions and activities on and involving the internet, World Wide Web and cyberspace.

Every action and reaction in cyberspace has some legal and cyber legal perspectives. Cyber law encompasses laws relating to –

- ➢ **Cyber crimes**
- ➢ **Electronic and digital signatures**
- ➢ **Intellectual property**
- ➢ **Data protection and privacy**

History of Internet and World Wide Web

The Internet is a global system of interconnected computer networks that use the standardized Internet Protocol Suite (TCP/IP). It is a network of networks that consists of millions of private and public, academic, business, and government networks of local to global scope that are linked by copper wires, fiber-optic cables, wireless connections, and other technologies. The Internet carries a vast array of information resources and services, most notably the inter-linked hypertext documents of the World Wide Web (WWW) and the infrastructure to support electronic mail, in addition to popular services such as online chat, file transfer and file sharing, online gaming, and Voice over

Internet Protocol (VoIP) person-to-person communication via voice and video. The origins of the Internet dates back to the 1960s when the United States funded research projects of its military agencies to build robust, fault-tolerant and distributed computer networks. This research and a period of civilian funding of a new U.S. backbone by the National Science Foundation spawned worldwide participation in the development of new networking technologies and led to the commercialization of an international network in the mid 1990s, and resulted in the following popularization of countless applications in virtually every aspect of modern human life.

The terms Internet and World Wide Web are often used in everyday speech without much distinction. However, the Internet and the World Wide Web are not one and the same. The Internet is a global data communications system. It is a hardware and software infrastructure that provides connectivity between computers. In contrast, the Web is one of the services communicated via the Internet. It is a collection of interconnected documents and other resources, linked by hyperlinks and Uniform Resource Locator [URLs]. The World Wide Web was invented in 1989 by the English physicist Tim Berners-Lee, now the Director of the World Wide Web Consortium, and later assisted by Robert Cailliau, a Belgian computer scientist, while both were working at CERN in Geneva, Switzerland. In 1990, they proposed building a "web of nodes" storing "hypertext pages" viewed by "browsers" on a network and released that web in December.

Overall Internet usage has seen tremendous growth. From 2000 to 2009, the number of Internet users globally rose from 394 million to 1.858 billion. By 2010, 22 percent of the world's population had access to computers with 1 billion Google searches every day, 300 million Internet users reading blogs, and 2 billion videos viewed daily on YouTube.

After English (27%), the most requested languages on the World Wide Web are Chinese (23%), Spanish (8%), Japanese (5%), Portuguese and German (4% each), Arabic, French and Russian (3% each), and Korean (2%). By region, 42% of the world's Internet users are based in Asia, 24% in Europe, 14% in North America, 10% in Latin America and the Caribbean taken together, 6% in Africa, 3% in the Middle East and 1% in Australia/Oceania.

CYBERSPACE

Cyberspace can be defined as an intricate environment that involves interactions between people, software, and services. It is maintained by the worldwide distribution of information and communication technology devices and networks.

With the benefits carried by the technological advancements, the cyberspace today has become a common pool used by citizens, businesses, critical information infrastructure, military and governments in a fashion that makes it hard to induce clear boundaries among these different groups. The cyberspace is anticipated to become even more complex in the upcoming years, with the increase in networks and devices connected to it.

CYBERSECURITY

Cybersecurity denotes the technologies and procedures intended to safeguard computers, networks, and data from unlawful admittance, weaknesses, and attacks transported through the Internet by cyber delinquents.

ISO 27001 (ISO27001) is the international Cybersecurity Standard that delivers a model for creating, applying, functioning, monitoring, reviewing, preserving, and improving an Information Security Management System.

The Ministry of Communication and Information Technology under the government of India provides a strategy outline called the National Cybersecurity Policy. The purpose of this government body is to protect the public and private infrastructure from cyber-attacks.

CYBERSECURITY POLICY

The cybersecurity policy is a developing mission that caters to the entire field of Information and Communication Technology (ICT) users and providers. It includes –
- Home users
- Small, medium, and large Enterprises
- Government and non-government entities

It serves as an authority framework that defines and guides the activities associated with the security of cyberspace. It allows all sectors and organizations in designing suitable cybersecurity policies to meet their requirements. The policy provides an outline to effectively protect information, information systems and networks.

It gives an understanding into the Government's approach and strategy for security of cyber space in the country. It also sketches some pointers to allow collaborative working across the public and private sectors to safeguard information and information systems. Therefore, the aim of this policy is to create a cybersecurity framework, which leads to detailed actions and programs to increase the security carriage of cyberspace.

CYBER CRIME AND CYBER LAW

We can define "Cyber Crime" as any malefactor or other offences where electronic communications or information systems, including any device or the Internet or both or more of them are involved [5].

We can define "Cyber law" as the legal issues that are related to utilize of communications technology, concretely "cyberspace", i.e. the Internet. It is an endeavor to integrate the challenges presented by human action on the Internet with legacy system of laws applicable to the physical world.

Cyber Crime
Sussman and Heuston first proposed the term "Cyber Crime" in the year 1995. Cybercrime cannot be described as a single definition, it is best considered as a collection of acts or conducts. These acts are based on the material offence object that affects the computer data or systems. These are the illegal acts where a digital device or information system is a tool or a target or it can be the combination of both. The cybercrime is also known as electronic crimes, computer-related crimes, e-crime, high-technology crime, information age crime etc.

In simple term we can describe "Cyber Crime" are the offences or crimes that takes place over electronic communications or information systems. These types of crimes are basically the illegal activities in which a computer and a network are involved. Due of the development of the internet, the volumes of the cybercrime activities are also increasing because when committing a crime there is no longer a need for the physical present of the criminal.

The unusual characteristic of cybercrime is that the victim and the offender may never come into direct contact. Cybercriminals often opt to operate from countries with nonexistent or weak cybercrime laws in order to reduce the chances of detection and prosecution.

There is a myth among the people that cyber crimes can only be committed over the cyberspace or the internet. In fact cyber crimes can also be committed without ones involvement in the cyber space, it is not necessary that the cyber criminal should remain present online. Software privacy can be taken as an example.

History of Cyber Crime
The first Cyber Crime was recorded within the year 1820. The primeval type of computer has been in Japan, China and India since 3500 B.C, but Charles Babbage's analytical engine is considered as the time of present day computers. In the year 1820, in France a textile manufacturer named Joseph-Marie Jacquard created the loom. This device allowed a series of steps that was continual within the weaving of special fabrics or materials. This resulted in an exceeding concern among the Jacquard's workers that their livelihoods as well as their traditional employment were being threatened, and prefer to sabotage so as to discourage Jacquard so that the new technology cannot be utilized in the future [7].

Evolution of Cyber Crime
The cyber crime is evolved from Morris Worm to the ransomware. Many countries including India are working to stop such crimes or attacks, but these attacks are continuously changing and affecting our nation.

Table: Evolution of Cyber Crime

Years	Types of Attacks
1997	Cyber crimes and viruses initiated, that includes Morris Code worm and other.
2004	Malicious code, Torjan, Advanced worm etc.
2007	Identifying thief, Phishing etc.
2010	DNS Attack, Rise of Botnets, SQL attacks etc
2013	Social Engineering, DOS Attack, BotNets, Malicious Emails, Ransomware attack etc.
Present	Banking Malware, Keylogger, Bitcoin wallet, Phone hijacking, Anroid hack, Cyber warfare etc.

Classifications of Cyber Crime

1. Cyber Crime against individuals: Crimes that are committed by the cyber criminals against an individual or a person. A few cyber crime against individuals are:

Email spoofing: This technique is a forgery of an email header. This means that the message appears to have received from someone or somewhere other than the genuine or actual source. These tactics are usually used in spam campaigns or in phishing, because people are probably going to open an electronic mail or an email when they think that the email has been sent by a legitimate source.

Spamming: Email spam which is otherwise called as junk email. It is unsought mass message sent through email. The uses of spam have become popular in the mid 1990s and it is a problem faced by most email users now a days. Recipient's email addresses are obtained by spam bots, which are automated programs that crawls the internet in search of email addresses. The spammers use spam bots to create email distribution lists. With the expectation of receiving a few number of respond a spammer typically sends an email to millions of email addresses.

Cyber defamation: Cyber defamation means the harm that is brought on the reputation of an individual in the eyes of other individual through the cyber space [9]. The purpose of making defamatory statement is to bring down the reputation of the individual.

IRC Crime (Internet Relay Chat): IRC servers allow the people around the world to come together under a single platform which is sometime called as rooms and they chat to each other.

Cyber Criminals basically uses it for meeting.
Hacker uses it for discussing their techniques.
Paedophiles use it to allure small children.

A few reasons behind IRC Crime:
Chat to win ones confidence and later starts to harass sexually, and then blackmail people for ransom, and if the victim denied paying the amount, criminal starts threatening to upload victim's nude photographs or video on the internet.

A few are paedophiles, they harass children for their own benefits.

A few uses IRC by offering fake jobs and sometime fake lottery and earns money .
Phishing: In this type of crimes or fraud the attackers tries to gain information such as login information or account's information by masquerading as a reputable individual or entity in various communication channels or in email.

Some other cyber crimes against individuals includes-Net extortion, Hacking, Indecent exposure, Trafficking, Distribution, Posting, Credit Card, Malicious code etc. The potential harm of such a malefaction to an individual person can scarcely be bigger.

2. Cyber Crime against property: These types of crimes includes vandalism of computers, Intellectual (Copyright, patented, trademark etc) Property Crimes, Online threatening etc. Intellectual property crime includes:

- **Software piracy:** It can be describes as the copying of software unauthorizedly.
- **Copyright infringement:** It can be described as the infringements of an individual or organization's copyright. In simple term it can also be describes as the using of copyright materials unauthorizedly such as music, software, text etc.
- **Trademark infringement:** It can be described as the using of a service mark or trademark unauthorizedly.

3. Cyber Crime against organization: Cyber Crimes against organization are as follows:

- **Unauthorized changing** or deleting of data.
- **Reading or copying** of confidential information unauthorizedly, but the data are neither being change nor deleted.
- **DOS attack:** In this attack, the attacker floods the servers, systems or networks with traffic in order to overwhelm the victim resources and make it infeasible or difficult for the users to use them [11].
- **Email bombing:** It is a type of Net Abuse, where huge numbers of emails are sent to an email address in order to overflow or flood the mailbox with mails or to flood the server where the email address is.
- **Salami attack:** The other name of Salami attack is Salami slicing. In this attack, the attackers use an online database in order to seize the customer's information like bank details, credit card details etc. Attacker deduces very little amounts

from every account over a period of time. In this attack, no complaint is file and the hackers remain free from detection as the clients remain unaware of the slicing.

- Some other cyber crimes against organization includes-Logical bomb, Torjan horse, Data diddling etc.

4. Cyber Crime against society: Cyber Crime against society includes:
Forgery: Forgery means making of false document, signature, currency, revenue stamp etc.
Web jacking: The term Web jacking has been derived from hi jacking. In this offence the attacker creates a fake website and when the victim opens the link a new page appears with the message and they need to click another link. If the victim clicks the link that looks real he will redirected to a fake page. These types of attacks are done to get entrance or to get access and controls the site of another. The attacker may also change the information of the victim's webpage

Cyber Crime on the rise

As per the cyber crime data maintained by the National Crime Records Bureau (NCRB), a total of 217, 288, 420 and 966 Cyber Crime cases were registered under the Information Technology Act, 2000 during 2007, 2008, 2009 and 2010 respectively. Also, a total of 328, 176, 276 and 356 cases were registered under Cyber Crime related Sections of Indian Penal Code (IPC) during 2007, 2008, 2009 and 2010 respectively. A total of 154, 178, 288 and 799 persons were arrested under Information Technology Act 2000 during 2007-2010. A total number of 429, 195, 263 and 294 persons were arrested under Cyber Crime related Sections of Indian Penal Code (IPC) during 2007-2010.

As per 2011 NCRB figures, there were 1,791 cases registered under the IT Act during the year 2011 as compared to 966 cases during the previous year (2010) thereby reporting an increase of 85.4% in 2011 over 2010.

Of this, 19.5% cases (349 out of 1,791 cases) were reported from Andhra Pradesh followed by Maharashtra (306), Kerala (227), Karnataka (151) and Rajasthan (122). And 46.1% (826 cases) of the total 1,791 cases registered under IT Act, 2000 were related to loss/damage to computer resource/utility reported under hacking with computer systems.

According to NCRB, the police have recorded less than 5,000—only 4,829 cases and made fewer arrests (3,187) between 2007 and 2011, under both the Information Technology (IT) Act as well as the Indian Penal Code (IPC).

And convictions remain in single digits, according to lawyers. Only 487 persons were arrested for committing such offences during the year 2011. There were 496 cases of obscene publications/transmission in electronic form during the year 2011 wherein 443 persons were arrested.

Out of total 157 cases relating to hacking under Sec. 66(2), most of the cases (23 cases) were reported from Karnataka followed by Kerala (22) and Andhra Pradesh (20 cases). And 20.4% of the 1184 persons arrested in cases relating to IT Act, 2000 were from Andhra Pradesh (242) followed by Maharashtra (226).

The age-wise profile of persons arrested in cyber crime cases under the IT Act, 2000 showed that 58.6% of the offenders were in the age group 18–30 years (695 out of 1184) and 31.7% of the offenders were in the age group 30-45 years (376 out of 1184). Madhya Pradesh (10), Maharashtra (4), Kerala (3) and Delhi (2) reported offenders whose age was below 18 years.

Meanwhile, a total of 422 cases were registered under the Indian Penal Code or IPC Sections during the year 2011 as compared to 356 such cases during 2010 thereby reporting an increase of 18.5%. Maharashtra reported maximum number of such cases (87 out of 422 cases i.e. 20.6%) followed by Chhattisgarh 18.0% (76 cases) and Delhi 11.6% (49 Cases).

Majority of the crimes out of total 422 cases registered under IPC fall under 2 categories--forgery (259) and Criminal Breach of Trust or fraud (118). Although such offences fall under the traditional IPC crimes, these cases had the cyber overtones wherein computer, Internet or its enabled services were present in the crime and hence they were categorised as Cyber Crimes under IPC.

Crime head-wise and age-wise profile of the offenders arrested under Cyber Crimes (IPC) for the year 2011 reveals that offenders involved inforgery cases were more in the age-group of 18-30 (46.5%) (129 out of 277). 50.4% of the persons arrested under Criminal Breach of Trust/Cyber Fraud offences were in the age group 30-45 years (65 out of 129).

Meanwhile 9 out of 88 mega cities did not report any case of cyber crime i.e., neither under the IT Act nor under IPC Sections during the year 2011.

And 53 mega cities have reported 858 cases under IT Act and 200 cases under various sections of IPC. There was an increase of 147.3% (from 347 cases in 2009 to 858 cases in 2011) in cases under IT Act as compared to previous year (2010), and an increase of 33.3% (from 150 cases in 2010 to 200 cases in 2011) of cases registered under various sections of IPC.

Bangalore (117), Vishakhapatnam (107), Pune (83), Jaipur (76), Hyderabad (67) and Delhi (City) (50) have reported high incidence of cases (500 out of 858 cases) registered under IT Act, accounting for more than half of the cases (58.3%) reported under the IT Act. Delhi City has reported the highest incidence (49 out of 200) of cases reported under IPC sections accounting for 24.5% followed by Mumbai (25 or 12.5%).

A major programme has been initiated on development of cyber forensics specifically cyber forensic tools, setting up of infrastructure for investigation and training of the users, particularly police and judicial officers in use of this tool to collect and analyze the digital evidence and present them in Court.

Indian Computer Emergency Response Team (CERT-In) and Centre for Development of Advanced Computing (CDAC) are involved in providing basic and advanced training of Law Enforcement Agencies, Forensic labs and judiciary on the procedures and methodology of collecting, analyzing and presenting digital evidence.

Cyber forensic training lab has been set up at Training Academy of Central Bureau of Investigation (CBI) to impart basic and advanced training in Cyber Forensics and Investigation of Cyber Crimes to Police Officers associated with CBI. In addition, Government has set up cyber forensic training and investigation labs in Kerala, Assam, Mizoram, Nagaland, Arunachal Pradesh, Tripura, Meghalaya, Manipur and Jammu & Kashmir.

In collaboration with Data Security Council of India (DSCI), NASSCOM, Cyber Forensic Labs have been set up at Mumbai, Bengaluru, Pune and Kolkata. DSCI has organized 112 training programmes on Cyber Crime Investigation and awareness and a total of 3680 Police officials, judiciary and Public prosecutors have been trained through these programmes.

Indian Computer Emergency Response Team (CERT-In) issues alerts, advisories and guidelines regarding cyber security threats and measures to be taken to prevent cyber incidents and enhance security of Information Technology systems.

Cyber Crime Statistics in India

The latest NCRB (National Crime Record Bureau) publication of 2017 indicates an increasing incidence of cybercrime in India..

Cyber crime cases registered and arrests made, 2010-13

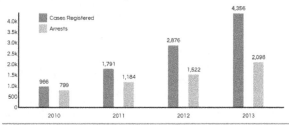

Created using www.datavisu.al

Crime Head	Crime Incidence			Percentage Variation	
	2014	2015	2016	2014 - 2015	2015 – 2016
Total Cyber Crimes	9,622	11,592	12,317	20.5%	6.3%

The aforesaid figures indicate an upsurge in rate of cybercrime over the years, however, the percentage variation in 2015-2016 is lower than the percentage variation in 2014-2015.

State-wise data is as follows;

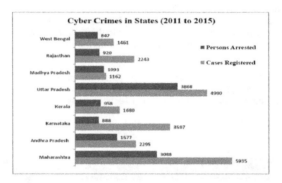

The Times Of India Newspaper, Delhi Edition, 22 July 2017

New Delhi, July 22: In India, at least one cyber attack was reported every 10 minutes in the first six months of 2017. In 2017, as per the Indian Computer Emergency Response Team (CERT-In), a total of 27,482 cases of cybercrimes have been reported across the world. These include phishing, site intrusion, virus, and ransomware. The cyber experts told *Times of India* that with the programs such as Digital India in place, more Indians are surfing the Internet and hence, it is crucial to put critical infrastructure in place to predict and prevent cybercrimes.

With the high percentage of cybercrime coming forward this year, the numbers are expected to shoot up in future. Mirza Faizan Asad, a cyber crime expert was quoted by TOI saying: " The government is making an effort to reduce online crimes but the firms and the individuals need to be ready with a strong team that is programmed for preventing such crimes." He added: "It is not just enough to make efforts at the government level, which is, in some sense happening, but cybercrime affects hundreds of individual systems and firms, all of whom need to be ready with specialised teams."

A total of 1.71 lakh cybercrimes were reported in India in the past three-and-a-half years. The number of crimes that have been reported so far (27,482) indicates that the total number is likely to cross 50,000 by December.

CYBER LAW
Cyber Law took birth in order to take control over the crimes committed through the internet or the cyberspace or through the uses of computer resources.

Description of the lawful issues that are related to the uses of communication or computer technology can be termed as Cyber Law.

Need for Cyber law
In today's techno-savvy environment, the world is becoming more and more digitally sophisticated and so are the crimes. Internet was initially developed as a research and information sharing tool and was in an unregulated manner. As the time passed by it became more transactional with e-business, e-commerce, e-governance and e-procurement etc. All legal issues related to internet crime are dealt with through cyber laws. As the number of internet users is on the rise, the need for cyber laws and their application has also gathered great momentum. In today's highly digitalized world, almost everyone is affected by cyber law. For example:

o Almost all transactions in shares are in demat form.

o Almost all companies extensively depend upon their computer networks and keep their valuable data in electronic form.

o Government forms including income tax returns, company law forms etc. are now filled in electronic form.

o Consumers are increasingly using credit cards for shopping.

o Most people are using email, cell phones and SMS messages for communication.

o Even in "non-cyber crime" cases, important evidence is found in computers / cell phones e.g. in cases of divorce, murder, kidnapping, tax evasion, organized crime, terrorist operations, counterfeit currency etc.

o Cyber crime cases such as online banking frauds, online share trading fraud, source code theft, credit card fraud, tax evasion, virus attacks, cyber sabotage, phishing attacks, email hijacking, denial of service, hacking, pornography etc are becoming common.

o Digital signatures and e-contracts are fast replacing conventional methods of transacting business.

Technology is never a disputed issue but for whom and at what cost has been the issue in the ambit of governance. The cyber revolution holds the promise of quickly reaching the masses as opposed to the earlier technologies, which had a trickledown effect. Such a promise and potential can only be realized with an appropriate legal regime based on a given socio-economic matrix.

Important terms related to Cyber Law

"**Access**" with its grammatical variations and cognate expressions means gaining entry into, instructing or communicating with the logical, arithmetical, or memory function resources of a computer, computer system or computer network. (Sec.2(1)(a) of IT Act, 2000)

"**Addressee**" means a person who is intended by the originator to receive the electronic record but does not include any intermediary. (Sec.2(1)(b) of IT Act, 2000)

"**Affixing Electronic Signature**" with its grammatical variations and cognate expressions means adoption of any methodology or procedure by a person for the purpose of authenticating an electronic record by means of Electronic Signature. (Sec.2(1)(d) of IT Act, 2000)

"**Asymmetric Crypto System**" means a system of a secure key pair consisting of a private key for creating a digital signature and a public key to verify the digital signature. (Sec.2(1)(f) of IT Act, 2000)

"**Certifying Authority**" means a person who has been granted a license to issue a Electronic Signature Certificate under section 24. (Sec.2(1)(g) of IT Act, 2000)

"**Communication Device**" means Cell Phones, Personal Digital Assistance (Sic), or combination of both or any other device used to communicate, send or transmit any text, video, audio, or image. (Sec.2(1)(ha) of IT Act, 2000)

"**Computer**" means any electronic, magnetic, optical or other high-speed data processing device or system which performs logical, arithmetic, and memory functions by manipulations of electronic, magnetic or optical impulses, and includes all input, output, processing, storage, computer software, or communication facilities which are connected or related to the computer in a computer system or computer network (Sec.2(1)(i) of IT Act, 2000)

"**Computer Network**" means the interconnection of one or more Computers or Computer systems or Communication device through-

the use of satellite, microwave, terrestrial line, wire, wireless or other communication media; and terminals or a complex consisting of two or more interconnected computers or communication device whether or not the interconnection is continuously maintained. (Sec.2(1)(j) of IT Act, 2000)

"**Computer Resource**" means computer, communication device, computer system, computer network, data, computer database or software. (Sec.2(1)(k) of IT Act, 2000)

"**Computer System**" means a device or collection of devices, including input and output support devices and excluding calculators which are not programmable and capable of being used in conjunction with external files, which contain computer programmes, electronic instructions, input data, and output data, that performs logic, arithmetic, data storage and retrieval, communication control and other functions. (Sec.2(1)(l) of IT Act,

2000)

"**Cyber cafe**" means any facility from where access to the Internet is offered by any person in the ordinary course of business to the members of the public. (Sec.2(1)(na) of IT Act, 2000)

"**Cyber Security**" means protecting information, equipment, devices, computer, computer resource, communication device and information stored therein from unauthorized access, use, disclosure, disruption, modification or destruction (Sec.2(1)(nb) of IT Act, 2000)

"**Data**" means a representation of information, knowledge, facts, concepts or instructions which are being prepared or have been prepared in a formalized manner, and is intended to be processed, is being processed or has been processed in a computer system or computer network and may be in any form
(including computer printouts magnetic or optical storage media, punched cards, punched tapes) or stored internally in the memory of the computer. (Sec.2(1)(o) of IT Act, 2000)

"**Digital Signature**" means authentication of any electronic record by a subscriber by means of an electronic method or procedure in accordance with the provisions of section 3. (Sec.2(1)(p) of IT Act, 2000)

"**Electronic Form**" with reference to information means any information generated, sent, received or stored in media, magnetic, optical, computer memory, micro film, computer generated micro fiche or similar device. (Sec.2(1)(r) of IT Act, 2000)

"**Electronic Record**" means data, record or data generated, image or sound stored, received or sent in an electronic form or micro film or computer generated micro fiche. (Sec.2(1)(t) of IT Act, 2000)

"**Electronic signature**" means authentication of any electronic record by a subscriber by means of the electronic technique specified in the second schedule and includes digital signature. (Sec.2(1)(ta) of IT Act, 2000)

"**Function**", in relation to a computer, includes logic, control, arithmetical process, deletion, storage and retrieval and communication or telecommunication from or within a computer. (Sec.2(1)(u) of IT Act, 2000)

"**Information**" includes data, message, text, images, sound, voice, codes, computer programmes, software and databases or micro film or computer generated micro fiche. (Sec.2(1)(v) of IT Act, 2000)

"**Intermediary**" with respect to any particular electronic records, means any person who on behalf of another person receives, stores or transmits that record or provides any service with respect to that record and includes telecom service providers, network service providers, internet service providers, web hosting service providers, search engines, online payment sites, online-auction sites, online market places and cyber cafes. (Sec.2(1)(w) of IT Act, 2000)

"**Key Pair**", in an asymmetric crypto system, means a private key and its mathematically related public key, which are so related that the public key can verify a digital signature created by the private key. (Sec.2(1)(x) of IT Act, 2000)

"**Originator**" means a person who sends, generates, stores or transmits any electronic message or causes any electronic message to be sent, generated, stored or transmitted to any other person but does not include an intermediary. (Sec.2(1)(za) of IT Act, 2000)

"**Private Key**" means the key of a key pair used to create a digital signature. (Sec.2(1)(zc) of IT Act, 2000)

"**Public Key**" means the key of a key pair used to verify a digital signature and listed in the Digital Signature Certificate. (Sec.2(1)(zd) of IT Act, 2000)

"**Secure System**" means computer hardware, software, and procedure that -:
- are reasonably secure from unauthorized access and misuse;

- provide a reasonable level of reliability and correct operation;

- are reasonably suited to performing the intended functions; and

- adhere to generally accepted security procedures. (Sec.2(1)(ze) of IT Act, 2000)

"**Subscriber**" means a person in whose name the Electronic Signature Certificate is issued. (Sec.2(1)(zg) of IT Act, 2000)

2

CYBER LAW IN INDIA

In India, cyber laws are contained in the Information Technology Act, 2000 ("IT Act") which came into force on October 17, 2000. The main purpose of the Act is to provide legal recognition to electronic commerce and to facilitate filing of electronic records with the Government.

The following Act, Rules and Regulations are covered under cyber laws:

- Information Technology Act, 2000

- Information Technology (Certifying Authorities) Rules, 2000

- Information Technology (Security Procedure) Rules, 2004

- Information Technology (Certifying Authority) Regulations, 2001

History of Cyber Law in India

The information Technology Act is an outcome of the resolution dated 30th January 1997 of the General Assembly of the United Nations, which adopted the Model Law on Electronic Commerce, adopted the Model Law on Electronic Commerce on International Trade Law. This resolution recommended, inter alia, that all states give favourable consideration to the said Model Law while revising enacting new law, so that uniformity may be observed in the laws, of the various cyber-nations, applicable to alternatives to paper based methods of communication and storage of information.

The Department of Electronics (DoE) in July 1998 drafted the bill. However, it could only be introduced in the House on December 16, 1999 (after a gap of almost one and a half years) when the new IT Ministry was formed. It underwent substantial alteration, with the Commerce Ministry making suggestions related to e-commerce and matters pertaining to World Trade Organization (WTO) obligations. The Ministry of Law and Company Affairs then vetted this joint draft.

After its introduction in the House, the bill was referred to the 42-member Parliamentary Standing Committee following demands from the Members. The Standing Committee made several suggestions to be incorporated into the bill.

However, only those suggestions that were approved by the Ministry of Information Technology were incorporated. One of the suggestions that was highly debated upon was that a cyber café owner must maintain a register to record the names and addresses of all people visiting his café and also a list of the websites that they surfed. This suggestion was made as an attempt to curb cyber crime and to facilitate speedy locating of a cyber criminal. However, at the same time it was ridiculed, as it would invade upon a net surfer's privacy and would not be economically viable. Finally, this suggestion was dropped by the IT Ministry in its final draft.

The Union Cabinet approved the bill on May 13, 2000 and on May 17, 2000, both the houses of the Indian Parliament passed the Information Technology Bill. The Bill received the assent of the President on 9th June 2000 and came to be known as the Information Technology Act, 2000. The Act came into force on17[th] October 2000.

With the passage of time, as technology developed further and new methods of committing crime using Internet & computers surfaced, the need was felt to amend the IT Act, 2000 to insert new kinds of cyber offences and plug in other loopholes that posed hurdles in the effective enforcement of the IT Act, 2000.

This led to the passage of the Information Technology (Amendment) Act, 2008 which was made effective from 27 October 2009. The IT (Amendment) Act, 2008 has brought marked changes in the IT Act, 2000 on several counts.

Information Technology Act, 2000

Information Technology Act, 2000 is India's mother legislation regulating the use of computers, computer systems and computer networks as also data and information in the electronic format. This legislation has touched varied aspects pertaining to electronic authentication, digital (electronic) signatures, cyber crimes and liability of network service providers.

The Preamble to the Act states that it aims at providing legal recognition for transactions carried out by means of electronic data interchange and other means of electronic communication, commonly referred to as "electronic commerce", which involve the use of alternatives to paper-based methods of communication and storage of information and aims at facilitating electronic filing of documents with the Government agencies.

The IT Act of 2000 was developed to promote the IT industry, regulate e-commerce, facilitate e-governance and prevent cybercrime. The Act also sought to foster security practices within India that would serve the country in a global context. The Amendment was created to address issues that the original bill failed to cover and to accommodate further development of IT and related security concerns since the original law was passed.

The IT Act, 2000 consists of 90 sections spread over 13 chapters [Sections 91, 92, 93 and 94 of the principal Act were omitted by the Information Technology (Amendment) Act 2008 and has 2 schedules.[Schedules III and IV were omitted by the Information Technology (Amendment) Act 2008].

Rules notified under the Information Technology Act, 2000

The Information Technology (Reasonable security practices and procedures and sensitive personal data or information) Rules, 2011

The Information Technology (Electronic Service Delivery) Rules, 2011

The Information Technology (Intermediaries guidelines) Rules, 2011

The Information Technology (Guidelines for Cyber Cafe) Rules, 2011

The Cyber Appellate Tribunal (Salary, Allowances and other terms and conditions of service of Chairperson and Members) Rules, 2009

The Cyber Appellate Tribunal (Procedure for investigation of Misbehaviour or Incapacity of Chairperson and Members) Rules, 2009

The Information Technology (Procedure and Safeguards for Blocking for Access of Information by Public), 2009

The Information Technology (Procedure and Safeguards for interception, monitoring and decryption of information) Rules, 2009

The Information Technology (Procedure and Safeguard for Monitoring and Collecting Traffic Data or Information) Rules, 2009

The Information Technology (Use of electronic records and digital signatures) Rules, 2004

The Information Technology (Security Procedure) Rules, 2004

The Information Technology (Other Standards) Rules, 2003

The Information Technology (Certifying Authority) Regulations, 2001

Information Technology (Certifying Authorities) Rules, 2000

Overview of other laws amended by the IT Act, 2000

The Indian Penal Code of 1860 and the Indian Evidence Act of 1872 was amended by the IT Act of 2000 to keep in tune with the technological changes that were rising rapidly.

Indian Penal Code, 1860

Amendments related to IPC were contained in Sec.91 and the First Schedule of the IT Act, 2000. Pursuant to the enactment of the Information Technology (amendment) Act, 2008, Sec.91 was deleted and the provisions with regard to Indian Penal Code were mentioned in Part III of the amendment Act. The amendments made to the Indian Penal Code are as follows –

Amendment to Sec.4 –

In section 4, -

i) after clause (2), the following clause shall be inserted namely: - (3) any person in any place without and beyond India committing offence targeting a computer resource located in India

ii) for the Explanation, the following Explanation shall be substituted, namely:- (a) the word "offence" includes every act committed outside India which, if committed in India would be punishable under this code. (b) the expression "computer resource" shall have the meaning assigned to it in clause (k) of subsection (1) of section 2 of the Information Technology Act, 2000.

Amendment of Sec.40 –

In clause (2), after the figure "117", the figures "118,119 and 120" shall be inserted.

Amendment of Sec.118 –

In section 118, for the words "voluntarily conceals, by any act or illegal omission, the existence of a design", the words "voluntarily conceals by any act or omission or by the use of encryption or any other information hiding tool, the existence of a design" shall be substituted.

Amendment of Sec.119 –

In section 119, for the words "voluntarily conceals, by any act or illegal omission, the existence of a design", the words "voluntarily conceals by any act or omission or by the use of encryption or any other information hiding tool, the existence of a design" shall be substituted.

Amendment of Sec.464 –

In section 464, for the words "digital signature" wherever they occur, the words "electronic signature" shall be substituted.

Indian Evidence Act, 1872

Amendments related to the evidence Act were contained in Sec.92 and the Second Schedule of the IT Act, 2000. Pursuant to the enactment of the Information Technology (amendment) Act, 2008, Sec.92 was deleted and the provisions with regard to the Indian Evidence Act were mentioned in Part IV of the amendment Act.

Amendment of Sec.3 –

In section 3 relating to interpretation clause, in the paragraph appearing at the end, for the words "digital signature" and "Digital Signature Certificate", the words "Electronic signature" and "Electronic Signature Certificate" shall be respectively substituted.

Insertion of new Sec.45A – Opinion of Examiner of Electronic evidence –
45A: When in a proceeding, the Court has to form an opinion on any matter relating to any information transmitted or stored in any computer resource or any other electronic or digital form, the opinion of the Examiner of Electronic Evidence referred to in section 79A of the Information Technology Act, 2000, is a relevant fact. Explanation: For the purposes of this section, an Examiner of Electronic Evidence shall be an expert

Amendment of Sec.47A –
In section 47A,- (i) for the words "digital signature", the words "electronic signature" shall be substituted; (ii) for the words "Digital Signature Certificate", the words "Electronic Signature Certificate" shall be substituted.

Amendment of Sec.67A –
In section 67 A, - for the words "digital signature", the words "electronic signature" shall be substituted.

Amendment of Sec.85A –
In section 85A, for the words "digital signature", wherever they occur, the words "electronic signature" shall be substituted.

Amendment of Sec.85B –
In section 85B, - for the words "digital signature", wherever they occur, the words "electronic signature" shall be substituted.

Amendment of Sec.85C –
In section 85C, for the words "Digital Signature Certificate", the words "Electronic Signature Certificate" shall be substituted.

Amendment of Sec.90A –
In section 90A, the words "digital signature", at both places where they occur, the words "electronic signature" shall be substituted.

THE INFORMATION TECHNOLOGY ACT, 2000

The Information Technology Act was enacted with a view to give a fillip to the growth of electronic based transactions, to provide legal recognition for e-commerce and e-transactions, to facilitate e-governance, to prevent computer based crimes and ensure security practices and procedures in the context of widest possible use of information technology worldwide.

The Information Technology Act, 2000 (also known as ITA-2000, or the IT Act) is an Act of the Indian Parliament (No 21 of 2000) notified on 17 October 2000. It is the primary law in India dealing with cybercrime and electronic commerce. It is based on the United Nations Model Law on Electronic Commerce 1996 (UNCITRAL Model) recommended by the General Assembly of United Nations by a resolution dated 30 January 1997. The bill was passed in the budget session of 2000 and signed by President K. R. Narayanan on 9 May 2000. The bill was finalised by group of officials headed by then Minister of Information Technology Pramod Mahajan.

Information Technology Act, 2000

सत्यमेव जयते

the Act to provide legal recognition for transactions carried out by means of electronic data interchange and other means of electronic communication, commonly referred to as "electronic commerce", which involve the use of alternatives to paper-based methods of communication and storage of information, to nusta editing electronic filing of documents with the Government agencies and further to amend the Indian Penal Code, the Indian Evidence Act, 1872, the Bankers' Books Evidence Act, 1891 and the Reserve Bank of India Act, 1934 and for matters connected therewith or incidental thereto.

Reason for Framing IT Act

The IT Act 2000 attempts to change outdated laws and provides ways to deal with cyber crimes. Let's have an overview of the law where it takes a firm stand and has got successful in the reason for which it was framed.

1. The E-commerce industry carries out its business via transactions and communications done through electronic records . It thus becomes essential that such transactions be made legal . Keeping this point in the consideration, the IT Act 2000 empowers the government departments to accept filing, creating and retention of official documents in the digital format. The Act also puts forward the proposal for setting up

the legal framework essential for the authentication and origin of electronic records / communications through digital signature.

2. The Act legalizes the e-mail and gives it the status of being valid form of carrying out communication in India. This implies that e-mails can be duly produced and approved in a court of law , thus can be a regarded as substantial document to carry out legal proceedings.

3. The act also talks about digital signatures and digital records . These have been also awarded the status of being legal and valid means that can form strong basis for launching litigation in a court of law. It invites the corporate companies in the business of being Certifying Authorities for issuing secure Digital Signatures Certificates.

4. The Act now allows Government to issue notification on the web thus heralding e-governance.

5. It eases the task of companies of the filing any form, application or document by laying down the guidelines to be submitted at any appropriate office, authority, body or agency owned or controlled by the government. This will help in saving costs, time and manpower for the corporates.

6. The act also provides statutory remedy to the coporates in case the crime against the accused for breaking into their computer systems or network and damaging and copying the data is proven. The remedy provided by the Act is in the form of monetary damages, not exceeding Rs. 1 crore($200,000).

7. Also the law sets up the Territorial Jurisdiction of the Adjudicating Officers for cyber crimes and the Cyber Regulations Appellate Tribunal.

8. The law has also laid guidelines for providing Internet Services on a license on a non-exclusive basis.

Applicability of the Act

The Act will apply to the whole of India unless otherwise mentioned. It applies also to any offence or contravention there under committed outside India by any person.
The Act shall not apply to the following documents or transactions –

- A negotiable instrument as defined in Sec.13 of the Negotiable Instruments Act, 1881;

- A power of attorney as defined in Sec.1A of the Powers of Attorney Act,1882;

- A trust as defined in Section 3 of the Indian Trusts Act, 1882;

- A Will as defined in Sec.2(h) of the Indian Succession Act, 1925 including any other testamentary disposition by whatever name called;

- Any contract for the sale or conveyance of immovable property or any interest in such property.

Scheme of the Act

How the Act is structured: The Act totally has 13 chapters and 90 sections (the last four sections namely sections 91 to 94 in the ITA 2000 dealt with the amendments to the four Acts namely the Indian Penal Code 1860, The Indian Evidence Act 1872, The Bankers' Books Evidence Act 1891 and the Reserve Bank of India Act 1934). The Act begins with preliminary and definitions and from thereon the chapters that follow deal with authentication of electronic records, digital signatures, electronic signatures etc. The original Act contained 94 sections, divided in 13 chapters and 4 schedules. The laws apply to the whole of India. Persons of other nationalities can also be indicted under the law, if the crime involves a computer or network located in India.

Chapter – I – Preliminary

Chapter-II of the Act specifically stipulates that any subscriber may authenticate an electronic record by affixing his digital signature. It further states that any person can verify an electronic record by use of a public key of the subscriber.

Chapter-III of the Act details about Electronic Governance and provides inter alia amongst others that where any law provides that information or any other matter shall be in writing or in the typewritten or printed form, then, notwithstanding anything contained in such law, such requirement shall be deemed to have been satisfied if such information or matter is -
rendered or made available in an electronic form; and accessible so as to be usable for a subsequent reference. The said chapter also details the legal recognition of Digital Signatures.

Chapter-IV of the said Act gives a scheme for Regulation of Certifying Authorities. The Act envisages a Controller of Certifying Authorities who shall perform the function of exercising supervision over the activities of the Certifying Authorities as also laying down standards and conditions governing the Certifying Authorities as also specifying the various forms and content of Digital Signature Certificates. The Act recognizes the need for recognizing foreign Certifying Authorities and it further details the various provisions for the issue of license to issue Digital Signature Certificates.

Chapter–V– Secure electronic records and secure electronic   signatures (Sections 14 to 16)

Chapter – VI – Regulation of Certifying Authorities (Sections 17 to 34)

Chapter-VII of the Act details about the scheme of things relating to Digital Signature Certificates. The duties of subscribers are also enshrined in the said Act.

Chapter – VIII – Duties of Subscribers (Sections 40 to 42)

Chapter-IX of the said Act talks about penalties and adjudication for various offences. The penalties for damage to computer, computer systems etc. has been fixed as damages by way of compensation not exceeding Rs. 1,00,00,000 to affected persons. The Act talks of appointment of any officers not below the rank of a Director to the Government of India or an equivalent officer of state government as an Adjudicating Officer who shall adjudicate whether any person has made a contravention of any of the provisions of the said Act or rules framed there under. The said Adjudicating Officer has been given the powers of a Civil Court.

Chapter-X of the Act talks of the establishment of the Cyber Regulations Appellate Tribunal, which shall be an appellate body where appeals against the orders passed by the Adjudicating Officers, shall be preferred.

Chapter-XI of the Act talks about various offences and the said offences shall be investigated only by a Police Officer not below the rank of the Deputy Superintendent of Police. These offences include tampering with computer source documents, publishing of information, which is obscene in electronic form, and hacking.

Chapter XII – Intermediaries not to be liable in certain cases (Section 79)

Chapter XIIA – Examiner of Electronic Evidence (Section 79A)

Chapter XIII – Miscellaneous (Sections 80 to 90)

The Act also provides for the constitution of the Cyber Regulations Advisory Committee, which shall advice the government as regards any rules, or for any other purpose connected with the said act. The said Act also proposes to amend the Indian Penal Code, 1860, the Indian Evidence Act, 1872, The Bankers' Books Evidence Act, 1891, The Reserve Bank of India Act, 1934 to make them in tune with the provisions of the IT Act.

Advantages of IT Act

The IT Act 2000 attempts to change outdated laws and provides ways to deal with cyber crimes. We need such laws so that people can perform purchase transactions over the Net through credit cards without fear of misuse. The Act offers the much-needed legal framework so that information is not denied legal effect, validity or enforceability, solely on the ground that it is in the form of electronic records.

In view of the growth in transactions and communications carried out through electronic records, the Act seeks to empower government departments to accept filing, creating and retention of official documents in the digital format. The Act has also proposed a legal framework for the authentication and origin of electronic records / communications through digital signature.

From the perspective of e-commerce in India, the IT Act 2000 and its provisions contain many positive aspects. Firstly, the implications of these provisions for the e-businesses would be that email would now be a valid and legal form of communication in our country that can be duly produced and approved in a court of law.

Companies shall now be able to carry out electronic commerce using the legal infrastructure provided by the Act.

Digital signatures have been given legal validity and sanction in the Act.

The Act throws open the doors for the entry of corporate companies in the business of being Certifying Authorities for issuing Digital Signatures Certificates.

The Act now allows Government to issue notification on the web thus heralding e-governance.

The Act enables the companies to file any form, application or any other document with any office, authority, body or agency owned or controlled by the appropriate Government in electronic form by means of such electronic form as may be prescribed by the appropriate Government.

The IT Act also addresses the important issues of security, which are so critical to the success of electronic transactions. The Act has given a legal definition to the concept of secure digital signatures that would be required to have been passed through a system of a security procedure, as stipulated by the Government at a later date.

Under the IT Act, 2000, it shall now be possible for corporates to have a statutory remedy in case if anyone breaks into their computer systems or network and causes damages or copies data. The remedy provided by the Act is in the form of monetary damages, not exceeding Rs. 1 crore.

Weaknesses of IT Act

The IT Law 2000, though appears to be self sufficient, it takes mixed stand when it comes to many practical situations. It looses its certainty at many places like:

1. The law misses out completely the issue of Intellectual Property Rights, and makes no provisions whatsoever for copyrighting, trade marking or patenting of electronic information and data. The law even doesn't talk of the rights and liabilities of domain name holders , the first step of entering into the e-commerce.

2. The law even stays silent over the regulation of electronic payments gateway and segregates the negotiable instruments from the applicability of the IT Act , which may have major effect on the growth of e-commerce in India . It leads to make the banking and financial sectors irresolute in their stands .

3. The act empowers the Deputy Superintendent of Police to look up into the investigations and filling of charge sheet when any case related to cyber law is called. This approach is likely to result in misuse in the context of Corporate India as companies have public offices which would come within the ambit of "public place" under the Act. As a result, companies will not be able to escape potential harassment at the hands of the DSP.

4. Internet is a borderless medium ; it spreads to every corner of the world where life is possible and hence is the cyber criminal. Then how come is it possible to feel relaxed and secured once this law is enforced in the nation??

The Act initially was supposed to apply to crimes committed all over the world, but nobody knows how can this be achieved in practice , how to enforce it all over the world at the same time???

* The IT Act is silent on filming anyone's personal actions in public and then distributing it electronically. It holds ISPs (Internet Service Providers) responsible for third party data and information, unless contravention is committed without their knowledge or unless the ISP has undertaken due diligence to prevent the contravention .

* For example, many Delhi based newspapers advertise the massage parlors; and in few cases even show the 'therapeutic masseurs' hidden behind the mask, who actually are prostitutes. Delhi Police has been successful in busting out a few such rackets but then it is not sure of the action it can take...should it arrest the owners and editors of newspapers or wait for some new clauses in the Act to be added up?? Even the much hyped case of the arrest of Bajaj, the CEO of Bazee.com, was a consequence of this particular ambiguity of the law. One cannot expect an ISP to monitor what information their subscribers are sending out, all 24 hours a day.

Cyber law is a generic term, which denotes all aspects, issues and the legal consequences on the Internet, the World Wide Web and cyber space. India is the 12th nation in the world that has cyber legislation apart from countries like the US, Singapore, France, Malaysia and Japan .

But can the cyber laws of the country be regarded as sufficient and secure enough to provide a strong platform to the country's e-commerce industry for which they were meant?? India has failed to keep in pace with the world in this respect, and the consequence is not far enough from our sight; most of the big customers of India 's outsourcing company have started to re-think of carrying out their business in India. Bajaj's case has given the strongest blow in this respect and have broken India 's share in outsourcing market as a leader.

If India doesn't want to loose its position and wishes to stay as the world's leader forever in outsourcing market, it needs to take fast but intelligent steps to cover the glaring loopholes of the Act, or else the day is not far when the scenario of India ruling the world's outsourcing market will stay alive in the dreams only as it will be overtaken by its competitors.

Important provisions of the Act

1) Digital signature and Electronic signature

Digital Signatures provide a viable solution for creating legally enforceable electronic records, closing the gap in going fully paperless by completely eliminating the need to print documents for signing. Digital signatures enable the replacement of slow and expensive paper-based approval processes with fast, low-cost, and fully digital ones. The purpose of a digital signature is the same as that of a handwritten signature. Instead of using pen and paper, a digital signature uses digital keys (public-key cryptography). Like the pen and paper method, a digital signature attaches the identity of the signer to the document and records a binding commitment to the document. However, unlike a handwritten signature, it is considered impossible to forge a digital signature the way a written signature might be. In addition, the digital signature assures that any changes made to the data that has been signed cannot go undetected.

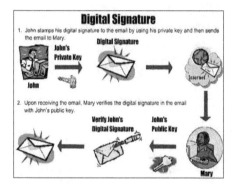

Digital signatures are easily transportable, cannot be imitated by someone else and can be automatically time-stamped. A digital signature can be used with any kind of message, whether it is encrypted or plaintext. Thus Digital Signatures provide the following three features:-

- Authentication - Digital signatures are used to authenticate the source of messages. The ownership of a digital signature key is bound to a specific user and thus a valid signature shows that the message was sent by that user.

- Integrity - In many scenarios, the sender and receiver of a message need assurance that the message has not been altered during transmission. Digital Signatures provide this feature by using cryptographic message digest functions.

- Non Repudiation – Digital signatures ensure that the sender who has signed the information cannot at a later time deny having signed it.

A handwritten signature scanned and digitally attached with a document does not qualify as a Digital Signature. An ink signature can be easily replicated from one document to another by copying the image manually or electronically. Digital Signatures cryptographically bind an electronic identity to an electronic document and the digital signature cannot be copied to another document.

Digital Signature under the IT Act, 2000

Digital signature means authentication of any electronic record by a subscriber by means of an electronic method or procedure in accordance with the provisions of section 3.

Section 3 deals with the conditions subject to which an electronic record may be authenticated by means of affixing digital signature which is created in two definite steps.

First, the electronic record is converted into a message digest by using a mathematical function known as 'Hash function' which digitally freezes the electronic record thus ensuring the integrity of the content of the intended communication contained in the electronic record. Any tampering with the contents of the electronic record will immediately invalidate the digital signature.

Secondly, the identity of the person affixing the digital signature is authenticated through the use of a private key which attaches itself to the message digest and which can be verified by anybody who has the public key corresponding to such private key. This will enable anybody to verify whether the electronic record is retained intact or has been tampered with since it was so fixed with the digital signature. It will also enable a person who has a public key to identify the originator of the message.

'Hash function' means an algorithm mapping or translation of one sequence of bits into another, generally smaller, set known as

"Hash Result" such that an electronic record yields the same hash result every time the algorithm is executed with the same electronic record as its input making it computationally infeasible to derive or reconstruct the original electronic record from the hash result produced by the algorithm; that two electronic records can produce the same hash result using the algorithm.

Digital signatures are a means to ensure validity of electronic transactions however who guarantees about the authenticity that such signatures are indeed valid or not false. In order that the keys be secure the parties must have a high degree of confidence in the public and private keys issued.

Digital Signature is not like our handwritten signature. It is a jumble of letters and digits. It looks something like this.

— BEGIN SIGNATURE—

Uz5xHz7DxFwvBAh24zPAQCmOYhT47gvuvzO0YbDA5txg5bN1Ni3hgPgnRz8FwxGUoDnj7awl7BwSBeW4
MSG7/3NS7oZyD/AWO1Uy2ydYD4UQt/w3d6D2Ilv3L8EO   IHIH
+r5K8Gpe5zK5CLV+zBKwGY47n6Bpi9JCYXz5YwXj4JxTT+y8=gy5N

— END SIGNATURE —

Electronic Signature

Electronic signature has also been dealt with under Section 3A of the IT Act, 2000. A subscriber can authenticate any electronic record by such electronic signature or electronic authentication technique which is considered reliable and may be specified in the Second Schedule.

Any electronic signature or electronic authentication technique will be considered reliable if-

- the signature creation data or the authentication data are, within the context in which they are used, linked to the signatory or , as the case may be, the authenticator and of no other person;

- the signature creation data or the authentication data were, at the time of signing, under the control of the signatory or, as the case may be, the authenticator and of no other person;

- any alteration to the electronic signature made after affixing such signature is detectable;

- any alteration to the information made after its authentication by electronic signature is detectable; and it fulfills such other conditions which may be prescribed.

An electronic signature will be deemed to be a secure electronic signature if-

- the signature creation data, at the time of affixing signature, was under the exclusive control of signatory and no other person; and

- the signature creation data was stored and affixed in such exclusive manner as may be prescribed. (Sec.15)

An Amendment to the IT Act in 2008 introduced the term electronic signatures. The implication of this Amendment is that it has helped to broaden the scope of the IT Act to include new techniques as and when technology becomes available for signing electronic records apart from Digital Signatures.

2. E-Governance

E-governance or Electronic Governance is dealt with under Sections 4 to 10A of the IT Act, 2000.

It provides for legal recognition of electronic records and Electronic signature and also provides for legal recognition of contracts formed through electronic means.

Filing of any form, application or other documents, creation, retention or preservation of records, issue or grant of any license or permit or receipt or payment in Government offices and its agencies may be done through the means of electronic form.

The Government may authorise any any service provider to set up, maintain and upgrade the computerized facilities and perform such other services as it may specify, by notification in the Official Gazette for efficient delivery of services to the public through electronic means. Service provider so authorized includes any individual, private agency, private company, partnership firm, sole proprietor form or any such other body or agency which has been granted permission by the appropriate Government to offer services through electronic means in accordance with the policy governing such service sector.

Where any law provides that documents, records or information should be retained for any specific period, then such documents, records or information retained in the electronic form will also be covered, if the information contained therein remains accessible; the electronic record is retained in the format in which it was originally generated, sent or received or in a format which can be demonstrated to represent accurately the information originally generated, sent or received and the details which will facilitate the identification of the origin, destination, date and time of dispatch or receipt of such electronic record are available in the electronic record.

Where any law provides for audit of documents, records or information, then that provision will also be applicable for audit of documents, records or information processed and maintained in electronic form.

Where any law provides that any rule, regulation, order, bye-law, notification or any other matter should be published in the Official Gazette, then, such requirement shall be deemed to have been satisfied if such rule, regulation, order, bye-law, notification or any other matter is published in the Official Gazette or Electronic Gazette.

However, the above mentioned provisions do not give a right to anybody to compel any Ministry or Department of the Government to use electronic means to accept, issue, create, retain and preserve any document or execute any monetary transaction.

The following are some of the eGovernance applications already using the Digital Signatures:-

- MCA21 – a Mission Mode project under NeGP (National e-governance plan) which is one of the first few e-Governance projects under NeGP to successfully implement Digital Signatures in their project

- Income Tax e-filing

- Indian Railway Catering and Tourism Corporation (IRCTC)

- Director General of Foreign Trade (DGFT)

- RBI Applications (SFMS : structured Financial Messaging System)

- National e-Governance Services Delivery Gateway (NSDG)

- eProcurement

- eOffice

- eDistrict applications of UP, Assam etc

3. Attribution, Acknowledgement and Dispatch of Electronic Records

Attribution of electronic records is dealt with under Sec.11 of the IT Act, 2000. An electronic record will be attributed to the originator - if it was sent by the originator himself; by a person who had the authority to act on behalf of the originator in respect of that electronic record; or by an information system programmed by or on behalf of the originator to operate automatically.

According to Section 12, the addressee may acknowledge the receipt of the electronic record either in a particular manner or form as desired by the originator and in the absence of such requirement, by communication of the acknowledgement to the addresses or by any conduct that would sufficiently constitute acknowledgement. Normally if the originator has stated that the electronic record will be binding only on receipt of the acknowledgement, then unless such acknowledgement is received, the record is not binding. However, if the acknowledgement is not received within the stipulated time period or in the absence of the time period, within a reasonable time, the originator may notify the addressee to send the acknowledgement, failing which the electronic record will be treated as never been sent. Time and place of dispatch and receipt of electronic record is covered under

Sec.13 of the IT Act, 2000. The dispatch of an electronic record occurs when it enters a computer resource outside the control of the originator. Unless otherwise agreed between the originator and the addressee, the time of receipt of an electronic record will be determined as follows, namely –

- if the addressee has designated a computer resource for the purpose of receiving electronic records –

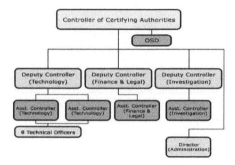

Receipt occurs at the time when the electronic record enters the designated computer resource; or if the electronic record is sent to a computer resource of the addressee that is not the designated computer resource, receipt occurs at the time when the electronic record is retrieved by the addressee;

- if the addressee has not designated a computer resource along with specified timings, if any, receipt occurs when the electronic record enters the computer resource of the addressee.

An electronic record is generally deemed to be dispatched at the place where the originator has his place of business, and is deemed to be received at the place where the addressee has his place of business.

- If the originator or the addressee has more than one place of business, the principal place of business will be the place of business. If the originator or the addressee does not have a place of business, his usual place of residence will be deemed to be the place of business. "Usual Place of Residence", in relation to a body corporate, means the place where it is registered.

4. Certifying Authorities

A Certifying Authority is a trusted body whose central responsibility is to issue, revoke, renew and provide directories of Digital Certificates. Certifying Authority means a person who has been granted a license to issue an Electronic Signature Certificate under section 24.

Provisions with regard to Certifying Authorities are covered under Chapter VI i.e. Sec.17 to Sec.34 of the IT Act, 2000. It contains detailed provisions relating to the appointment and powers of the Controller and Certifying Authorities.

Controller of Certifying Authorities (CCA)
The IT Act provides for the Controller of Certifying Authorities (CCA) to license and regulate the working of Certifying Authorities. The Certifying Authorities (CAs) issue digital signature certificates for electronic authentication of users.

The CCA certifies the public keys of CAs using its own private key, which enables users in the cyberspace to verify that a given certificate is issued by a licensed CA. For this purpose it operates, the Root Certifying Authority of India

(RCAI). The CCA also maintains the National Repository of Digital Certificates (NRDC), which contains all the certificates issued by all the CAs in the country.

The functions of the Controller are –

- to exercise supervision over the activities of the Certifying Authorities;

- certify public keys of the Certifying Authorities;

- lay down the standards to be maintained by the Certifying
- Authorities;

- specify the qualifications and experience which employees of the
- Certifying Authorities should possess;

- specify the conditions subject to which the Certifying Authorities shall conduct their business;

- specify the content of written, printed or visual material and advertisements that may be distributed or used in respect of a Electronic Signature Certificate and the Public Key;

- specify the form and content of a Electronic Signature Certificate and the key;

- specify the form and manner in which accounts shall be maintained by the Certifying Authorities;

- specify the terms and conditions subject to which auditors may be appointed and the remuneration to be paid to them;

- facilitate the establishment of any electronic system by a Certifying
- Authority either solely or jointly with other Certifying Authorities and regulation of such systems;

- specify the manner in which the Certifying Authorities shall conduct their dealings with the subscribers;

- resolve any conflict of interests between the Certifying Authorities and the subscribers;

- lay down the duties of the Certifying Authorities;

- maintain a data-base containing the disclosure record of every Certifying Authority containing such particulars as may be specified by regulations, which shall be accessible to the public.

Controller has the power to grant recognition to foreign certifying authorities with the previous approval of the Central Government, which will be subject to such conditions and restrictions imposed by regulations.

Root Certifying Authority of India (RCAI)
The Controller of Certifying Authorities (CCA) has established the RCAI under Section 18(b) of the IT Act to digitally sign the public keys of Certifying Authorities (CAs) in the country. The RCAI is operated as per the standards laid down under the Act.

The requirements fulfilled by the RCAI include the following:

- The licence issued to the CA is digitally signed by the CCA.
- All public keys corresponding to the signing private keys of a CA are digitally signed by the CCA.

That these keys are signed by the CCA can be verified by a relying party through the CCA's website or CA's own website.

The RCAI is operated using SmartTrust software. Authorized CCA personnel initiate and perform Root CA functions in accordance with the Certification Practice Statement of Root Certifying Authority of India. The term Root CA is used to refer to the total CA entity, including the software and its operations.

The RCAI root certificate is the highest level of certification in India. It is used to sign the public keys of the licensed CAs.

Certifying Authorities

Certifying Authorities (CAs) are responsible for issuing Digital Signature Certificates to the end users. In order to facilitate greater flexibility to Certifying

Authorities, the CCA has allowed the creation of sub-CAs. As per this model, a Certifying Authority can create a sub-CA to meet its business branding requirement. However the sub-CA will be part of the same legal entity as the CA. The sub-CA model will be based on the following principles:

- The CAs must not have more than one level of sub-CA.

- A sub-CA certificate issued by the CA is used for issuing end entity certificates.

- A CA with sub-CA must necessarily issue end entity certificates only through its sub-CA. The only exception will be for code signing and time stamping certificates, which may directly be issued by the CA.

The licensed Certifying Authorities (CAs) are –
- Safescrypt – a private Certifying Authority
- NIC – an organisation of Govt. of India, issuing certificates to
- Government organisations
- IDRBT – established by Reserve Bank of India for issuing certificates to the banking industry
- TCS – private certifying authority to issue certificates to individuals, company and government users
- MTNL
- Customs and Central Excise
- Code Solutions CA (GNFC)

- e-Mudhra

Who can become a Certifying Authority?

The following persons can apply for grant of a licence to issue Digital Signature Certificates, namely:-

- an individual, being a citizen of India and having a capital of five crores of rupees or more in his business or profession;

- a company having–
paid up capital of not less than five crores of rupees; and
net worth of not less than fifty crores of rupees:

No company in which the equity share capital held in aggregate by the Non-resident Indians, Foreign Institutional Investors, or foreign companies, exceeds forty-nine per cent of its capital, will be eligible for grant of licence.

In a case where the company has been registered under the Companies Act, 1956 during the preceding financial year or in the financial year during which it applies for grant of licence under the Act and whose main object is to act as Certifying Authority, the net worth referred to in sub-clause (ii) will be the aggregate net worth of its majority shareholders holding at least 51% of paid equity capital, being the Hindu Undivided

Family, firm or company. Majority shareholders should not include Non-resident Indian, foreign national, Foreign Institutional Investor and foreign company.

The majority shareholders of a company whose net worth has been determined on the basis of such majority shareholders should not sell or transfer its equity shares held in such company- unless such a company acquires or has its own net worth of not less than fifty crores of rupees and without prior approval of the Controller.

a firm having –
capital subscribed by all partners of not less than five crores of rupees; and net worth of not less than fifty crores of rupees.

No firm, in which the capital held in aggregate by any Non-resident Indian, and foreign national, exceeds forty-nine per cent of its capital, will be eligible for grant of licence.

In a case where the firm has been registered under the Indian Partnership Act, 1932 during the preceding financial year or in the financial year during which it applies for grant of licence under the Act and whose main object is to act as Certifying Authority, the net worth referred to in sub-clause (ii) should be the aggregate net worth of all of its partners. The partners should not include Non-resident Indian and foreign national. The partners of a firm whose net worth has been determined on the basis of such partners, should not sell or transfer its capital held in such firm - unless such firm has acquired or has its own net worth of not less than fifty crores of rupees and without prior approval of the Controller.

Central Government or a State Government or any of the Ministries or
Departments, Agencies or Authorities of such Governments

Submission of performance bond

The applicant should submit a performance bond or furnish a banker's guarantee from a scheduled bank in favour of the Controller in such form and in such manner as may be approved by the Controller for an amount of not less than five crores of rupees and the performance bond or banker's guarantee will remain valid for a period of six years from the date of its submission.

Submission of application

Every application for a licensed Certifying Authority should be made to the Controller in the form given in Schedule I of the Information Technology (Certifying Authorities) Rules, 2000.

Rule 10 of IT (Certifying Authorities) Rules, 2000 prescribes the following documents to be submitted along with the application –

- a Certification Practice Statement (CPS);

- a statement including the procedures with respect to identification of the applicant;

- a statement for the purpose and scope of anticipated Digital Signature

Certificate technology, management, or operations to be outsourced;

- certified copies of the business registration documents of Certifying
- Authority that intends to be licensed;

- a description of any event, particularly current or past insolvency, that could materially affect the applicant's ability to act as a Certifying Authority;

- an undertaking by the applicant that to its best knowledge and belief it can and will comply with the requirements of its Certification Practice Statement;

- an undertaking that the Certifying Authority's operation would not commence until its operation and facilities associated with the functions of generation, issue and management of Digital Signature Certificate are audited by the auditors and approved by the Controller in accordance with rule 20;

- an undertaking to submit a performance bond or banker's guarantee in accordance with sub-rule (2) of rule 8 within one month of Controller indicating his approval for the grant of licence to operate as a Certifying Authority;

- any other information required by the Controller.

Apart from the above mentioned documents, the following particulars also need to be furnished –
Company Profile/Experience of Individuals

For an individual, proof of capital of Rs. 5 crores or more in his business or profession

For a company/firm,
Proof of paid-up capital not less than Rs. 5 crores
Proof of net worth not less than Rs. 50 crores
Proof of Equity (Proof that equity share capital held in aggregate by NRIs, FIIs or foreign companies does not exceed 49% of its capital)

An undertaking to submit Performance Bond or Banker's Guarantee valid for six years from a

scheduled bank for an amount not less than
Rs. 5 crores in accordance with Rule 10(ii)(h) of the IT Act.

Crossed cheque or bank draft for Rs. 25,000/- (for fresh application) or Rs.5,000/- (for renewal) in favour of the Pay & Accounts Officer, DIT,
New Delhi. Both fees are non-refundable.

Certified true copies of the company's incorporation, articles of association etc.

Original business profile report with certification from Registrar of Companies.

Audited accounts for the past 3 years (if applicable).

The CA's Certification Practice Statement (CPS).

Technical specifications of the CA system and CA security policies, standards and infrastructure available/proposed and locations of facilities.

Information Technology and Security Policy proposed to be followed by the CA in its operations.

Statement addressing the manner in which the CA shall comply with the requirements stipulated in the IT Act, Rules and Regulations.

Organizational chart and details of all trusted personnel.

Date by which the applicant will be ready for audit to start. The application shall be deemed to have been received on this date for processing purposes.

Date by which commencement of CA operations is proposed.

An undertaking by the applicant that they will make payment to the Auditor appointed by the

CCA at the rate to be prescribed by the CCA.

The Controller reserves the right to call for any other information that may be required to process the application. The application for licence to operate as a Certifying Authority, including all supporting documents, must be submitted in triplicate. These should be in the form of three identical sets numbered 1, 2 and 3.

Issuance of licence

The Controller should within four weeks from the date of receipt of the application, after considering the documents accompanying the application and such other factors, as he may deem fit, grant or renew the licence or reject the application. In exceptional circumstances and for reasons to be recorded in writing, the period of four weeks may be extended to such period, not exceeding eight weeks in all as the Controller may deem fit.

If the application for licensed Certifying Authority is approved, then the applicant should submit a performance bond or furnish a banker's guarantee within one month from the date of such approval to the Controller and execute an agreement with the Controller binding himself to comply with the terms and conditions of the licence and the provisions of the Act and the rules made thereunder.

The licence will be valid for a period of five years from the date of its issue. The licence is not transferable. The provisions that are applicable for obtaining fresh licence will be applicable for renewal of licence also. Every application for renewal should be made atleast 45 days before the date of expiry.

Every Certifying Authority should display its licence at a conspicuous place of the premises in which it carries on its business.

Security Guidelines for Certifying Authorities
The Certifying Authorities will have the sole responsibility of integrity, confidentiality and protection of information and information assets employed in its operation, considering classification, declassification, labeling, storage, access and destruction of information assets according to their value, sensitivity and importance of operation.

Information Technology Security Guidelines and Security Guidelines for Certifying Authorities aimed at protecting the integrity, confidentiality and availability of service of Certifying Authority are given in Schedule-II and Schedule-III of the IT (Certifying Authorities) Rules, 2000.

The Certifying Authority should formulate its Information Technology and

Security Policy for operation complying with these guidelines and submit it to the Controller before commencement of operation. (Rule 19 of IT (Certifying Authorities) Rules, 2000)

Commencement of Operation by Licensed Certifying Authorities
The licensed Certifying Authority can commence its commercial operation of generation and issue of Digital Signature only after-

- it has confirmed to the Controller the adoption of Certification Practice Statement;

- it has generated its key pair, namely, private and corresponding public key, and submitted the public key to the Controller;

- the installed facilities and infrastructure associated with all functions of generation, issue and management of Digital Signature Certificate have been audited by the accredited auditor;

- it has submitted the arrangement for cross certification with other licensed Certifying Authorities within India to the Controller.

Procedures to be followed by Certifying Authorities
Every Certifying Authority should -

- make use of hardware, software, and procedures that are secure from intrusion and misuse:

- provide a reasonable level of reliability in its services which are reasonably suited to the performance of intended functions;

adhere to security procedures to ensure that the secrecy and privacy of the Electronic

Signature are assured;

be the repository of all Electronic Signature Certificates issued under the IT Act;

publish information regarding its practices, Electronic Signature

Certificates and current status of such certificates; and

observe such other standards as may be specified by regulations.

Audit of Certifying Authority

According to Rule 31 of the IT (Certifying Authorities) Rules, 2000, the

Certifying Authority should get its operations audited annually by an auditor and such audit should include —

- security policy and planning;
- physical security;
- technology evaluation;
- Certifying Authority's services administration;
- relevant Certification Practice Statement;
- compliance to relevant Certification Practice Statement;
- contracts/agreements;
- regulations prescribed by the Controller;
- policy requirements of Certifying Authorities Rules, 2000

The Certifying Authority should conduct half yearly audit of the Security Policy, physical security and planning of its operation and a quarterly audit of its repository.

The Certifying Authority should submit copy of each audit report to the Controller within four weeks of the completion of such audit and where irregularities are found, the Certifying Authority should take immediate appropriate action to remove such irregularities.

The auditor should be independent of the Certifying Authority being audited and should not be a software or hardware vendor which is, or has been providing services or supplying equipment to the said Certifying Authority. The auditor and the Certifying Authority should not have any current or planned financial, legal or other relationship, other than that of an auditor and the audited party.

Registration Authority (RA)

A Registration Authority (RA) acts as the verifier for the Certifying Authority before a Digital Signature Certificate is issued to a requestor. The Registration Authorities (RAs) process user requests, confirm their identities, and induct them into the user database.

5. Electronic Signature Certificates

Provisions relating to Electronic/Digital signature certificates are covered in Chapter VII i.e. Secs.35 to 39 of the IT Act, 2000 and Rules 23 to 30 of the IT (Certifying Authorities) Rules, 2000 and IT (Certifying Authority) Regulations, 2001.

A Digital Signature Certificate is an electronic document which uses a digital signature to bind together a public key with an identity — information such as the name of a person or an organization, their address, and so forth. The certificate can be used to verify that a public key belongs to the individual.

Digital certificates are the digital equivalent (i.e. electronic format) of physical or paper certificates. Examples of physical certificates are driver's licenses, passports or membership cards.

Digital Signature Certificates is issued by the Certifying Authority (CA). The CA is responsible for vetting all applications for Digital Signature Certificates, and once satisfied, generates a Digital Certificate by digitally signing the Public key of the individual along with other information using its own Private key.

The CCA has licensed eight Certifying Authorities in India to issue Digital

Signature Certificates to the end users. The National Informatics Centre issues Digital Signature Certificates primarily to the Government/ PSU's and

Statutory bodies. The Institute for Development of Research in Banking Technology (IDRBT) issues Digital Signature Certificates primarily to the banking and financial sector in India. The remaining CAs - Safescrypt, TCS,

MTNL, n(Code) Solutions and eMudhra issue Digital Signature Certificates to all end users across all domains. More than 16 lakh Digital Signature

Certificates have been issued by the different CA's in India.

Depending upon the requirement of assurance level and usage of Digital Signature Certificate, the following are the classes of Digital Signature

Certificates:-

- Class - 1 Certificate – issued to individuals/private subscribers to secure email messages.

- Class - 2 Certificates – issued as Managed Digital Certificates to employees/ partners/ affiliates/ customers of business and government organizations that are ready to assume the responsibility of verifying the accuracy of the information submitted by their employees/ partners/ affiliates/ customers.

- Class - 3 Certificates - issued to individuals, companies and government organizations. They can be used both for personal and commercial purposes. They are typically used for electronic commerce applications such as electronic banking, electronic data interchange (EDI), and membership-based on-line services, where security is a major concern.

Different types of digital signature certificates that are issued:–

Individual Digital Signature Certificates (Signing Certificates) - Individual Certificates serve to identify a person. It follows that the contents of this type of certificate include the full name and personal particulars of an individual. These certificates can be used for signing electronic documents and emails and implementing enhanced access control mechanisms for sensitive or valuable information.

Server Certificates - Server Certificates identify a server (computer). Hence, instead of a name of a person, server certificates contain the host name e.g. "https://nsdg.gov.in/" or the IP address. Server certificates are used for 1 way or 2 way SSL to ensure secure communication of data over the network.

Encryption Certificates - Encryption Certificates are used to encrypt the message. The Encryption Certificates use the Public Key of the recipient to encrypt the data so as to ensure data confidentiality during transmission of the message. Separate certificates for signatures and for encryption are available from different CAs.

Before the issue of the Digital Signature Certificate, the Certifying Authority should -

confirm that the user's name does not appear in its list of compromised users;

comply with the procedure as defined in his Certification Practice Statement including verification of identification and/or employment;

comply with all privacy requirements;

obtain a consent of the person requesting the Digital Signature Certificate, that the details of such Digital Signature Certificate can be published on a directory service.

The generation of the Digital Signature Certificate will involve:

receipt of an approved and verified Digital Signature Certificate request;

creating a new Digital Signature Certificate;

binding the key pair associated with the Digital Signature Certificate to a

Digital Signature Certificate owner;

Issuing the Digital Signature Certificate and the associated public key for operational use;

a distinguished name associated with the Digital Signature Certificate owner; and

a recognized and relevant policy as defined in Certification Practice Statement.

Certificate Revocation

Digital Signature Certificates are issued with a planned lifetime, which is defined through a validity start date and an explicit expiration date. A certificate may be issued with a validity of upto two years. Once issued, a Certificate is valid until its expiration date.

However, various circumstances may cause a certificate to become invalid prior to the expiration of the validity period. Such circumstances include change of name (for example, change the subject of a certificate due to an employee's change of name), change of association between subject and CA (for example, when an employee terminates employment with an organization), and compromise or suspected compromise of the corresponding private key. Under such circumstances, the issuing CA needs to revoke the certificate. In case a Digital Signature Certificate is compromised, one should immediately contact the respective CA to initiate revocation. The CA will then put the certificate in the Certificate Revocation List.

6. Duties of Subscribers

"Subscriber" means a person in whose name the Electronic Signature Certificate is issued.
Chapter VIII i.e. Secs.40 to 42 of the IT Act, 2000 deals with the duties of subscribers.
Where any Digital Signature Certificate, the public key of which corresponds to the private key of that subscriber which is to be listed in the Digital Signature Certificate has been accepted by a subscriber, the subscriber should generate that key pair by applying the security procedure.

A subscriber will be deemed to have accepted a Digital Signature Certificate if he publishes or authorizes the publication of a Digital Signature Certificate -

to one or more persons;
in a repository, or otherwise demonstrates his approval of the Digital Signature Certificate in any manner.

By accepting a Digital Signature Certificate the subscriber certifies to all who reasonably rely on the information contained in the Digital Signature Certificate that -
the subscriber holds the private key corresponding to the public key listed in the Digital Signature Certificate and is entitled to hold the same;
all representations made by the subscriber to the Certifying Authority and all material relevant to the information contained in the Digital Signature

Certificate are true;
all information in the Digital Signature Certificate that is within the knowledge of the subscriber is true.

Every subscriber should exercise reasonable care to retain control of the private key corresponding to the public key listed in his Digital Signature Certificate and take all steps to prevent its disclosure.

Where the private key corresponding to the public key listed in the Digital Signature Certificate has been compromised, the subscriber should communicate the same without any delay to the Certifying Authority. An application for revocation of the key pair should be made in Form online on the website of the concerned Certifying Authority to enable revocation and publication in the Certificate Revocation List. The Subscriber should encrypt this transaction by using the public key of the Certifying Authority. The transaction should be further authenticated with the private key of the subscriber even though it may have already been compromised. The subscriber will be liable till he has informed the Certifying Authority that the private key has been compromised.

7. Penalties and Offences
Following are the sections under IT Act, 2000

Section	Offence	Description	Penalty
65	Tampering with computer source documents	If a person knowingly or intentionally conceals, destroys or alters or intentionally or knowingly causes another to conceal, destroy or alter any computer source code used for a computer, computer programme, computer system or computer network, when the computer source code is required to be kept or maintained by law for the time being in force.	Imprisonment up to three years, or/and with fine up to ₹200,000
66	Hacking with computer system	If a person with the intent to cause or knowing that he is likely to cause wrongful loss or damage to the public or any person destroys or deletes or alters any information residing in a computer resource or diminishes its value or utility or affects it injuriously by any means, commits hack.	Imprisonment up to three years, or/and with fine up to ₹500,000
66B	Receiving stolen computer or communication device	A person receives or retains a computer resource or communication device which is known to be stolen or the person has reason to believe is stolen.	Imprisonment up to three years, or/and with fine up to ₹100,000
66C	Using password of another person	A person fradulently uses the password, digital signature or other unique identification of another person.	Imprisonment up to three years, or/and with fine up to ₹100,000
66D	Cheating using computer resource	If a person cheats someone using a computer resource or communication.	Imprisonment up to three years, or/and with fine up to ₹100,000
66E	Publishing private images of others	If a person captures, transmits or publishes images of a person's private parts without his/her consent or knowledge.	Imprisonment up to three years, or/and with fine up to ₹200,000
66F	Acts of cyberterrorism	If a person denies access to an authorised personnel to a computer resource, accesses a protected system or introduces contaminant into a system, with the intention of threatening the unity, integrity, sovereignty or security of India, then he commits cyberterrorism.	Imprisonment up to life.
67	Publishing information which is obscene in electronic form.	If a person publishes or transmits or causes to be published in the electronic form, any material which is lascivious or appeals to the prurient interest or if its effect is such as to tend to deprave and corrupt persons who are likely, having regard to all relevant circumstances, to read, see or hear the matter	Imprisonment up to five years, or/and with fine up to ₹1,000,000

Section	Offence	Description	Penalty
67A	Publishing images containing sexual acts	If a person publishes or transmits images containing a sexual explicit act or conduct.	Imprisonment up to seven years, or/and with fine up to ₹1,000,000
67B	Publishing child porn or predating children online	If a person captures, publishes or transmits images of a child in a sexually explicit act or conduct. If a person induces a child into a sexual act. A child is defined as anyone under 18.	Imprisonment up to five years, or/and with fine up to ₹1,000,000 on first conviction. Imprisonment up to seven years, or/and with fine up to ₹1,000,000 on second conviction.
67C	Failure to maintain records	Persons deemed as intermediatary (such as an ISP) must maintain required records for stipulated time. Failure is an offence.	Imprisonment up to three years, or/and with fine.
68	Failure/refusal to comply with orders	The Controller may, by order, direct a Certifying Authority or any employee of such Authority to take such measures or cease carrying on such activities as specified in the order if those are necessary to ensure compliance with the provisions of this Act, rules or any regulations made thereunder. Any person who fails to comply with any such order shall be guilty of an offence.	Imprisonment up to three years, or/and with fine up to ₹200,000
69	Failure/refusal to decrypt data	If the Controller is satisfied that it is necessary or expedient so to do in the interest of the sovereignty or integrity of India, the security of the State, friendly relations with foreign States or public order or for preventing incitement to the commission of any cognizable offence, for reasons to be recorded in writing, by order, direct any agency of the Government to intercept any information transmitted through any computer resource. The subscriber or any person in charge of the computer resource shall, when called upon by any agency which has been directed, must extend all facilities and technical assistance to decrypt the information. The subscriber or any person who fails to assist the agency referred is deemed to have committed a crime.	Imprisonment up to seven years and possible fine.
70	Securing access or attempting to secure access to a protected system	The appropriate Government may, by notification in the Official Gazette, declare that any computer, computer system or computer network to be a protected system. The appropriate Government may, by order in writing, authorise the persons who are authorised to access protected systems. If a person who secures access or attempts to secure access to a protected system, then he is committing an offence.	Imprisonment up to ten years, or/and with fine.
71	Misrepresentation	If anyone makes any misrepresentation to, or suppresses any material fact from, the Controller or the Certifying Authority for obtaining any license or Digital Signature Certificate	Imprisonment up to three years, or/and with fine up to ₹100,000

If a crime is committed on a computer or computer network in India by a person resident outside India, then can the offence be tried by the Courts in India?

According to Sec.1(2) of Information Technology Act, 2000, the Act extends to the whole of India and also applies to any offence or contravention committed outside India by any person. Further, Sec.75 of the IT Act, 2000 also mentions about the applicability of the Act for any offence or contravention committed outside India. According to this section, the Act will apply to an offence or contravention committed outside India by any person, if the act or conduct constituting the offence or contravention involves a computer, computer system or computer network located in India.

A Police officer not below the rank of Deputy Superintendent of Police should only investigate any offence under this Act. (Sec.78 of IT Act, 2000).

Without a duly signed extradition treaty or a multilateral cooperation arrangement, trial of such offences and conviction is a difficult proposition.

8. Intermediaries

Sec.79 deals with the immunity available to intermediaries. The Information Technology (Intermediaries guidelines) Rules, 2011 governs the duties of intermediaries.

"Intermediary" with respect to any particular electronic records, means any person who on behalf of another person receives, stores or transmits that record or provides any service with respect to that record and includes telecom service providers, network service providers, internet service providers, web hosting service providers, search engines, online payment sites, online-auction sites, online market places and cyber cafes.

Intermediary will not be liable for any third party information, data or communication link hosted by him. It will apply only if –

- the function of the intermediary is limited to providing access to a communication system over which information made available by third parties is transmitted or temporarily stored or hosted;

- the intermediary does not initiate the transmission or select the receiver of the transmission and select or modify the information contained in the transmission;

- the intermediary observes due diligence while discharging his duties.

The intermediary will be held liable if he conspired or abetted or aided or induced whether by threats or promise or otherwise in the commission of the unlawful act. He will also be liable if upon receiving actual knowledge or on being notified that any information, data or communication link residing in or connected to a computer resource controlled by it is being used to commit an unlawful act and it fails to expeditiously remove or disable access to that material.

The intermediary should observe the following due diligence while discharging his duties –

- The intermediary should publish the rules and regulations, privacy policy and user agreement for access-or usage of the intermediary's computer resource by any person.

- Such rules and regulations, terms and conditions or user agreement shall inform the users of computer resource not to host, display, upload, modify, publish, transmit, update or share any information.

- The intermediary should not knowingly host or publish any information or should not initiate the transmission, select the receiver of transmission, and select or modify the information contained in the transmission.

- The intermediary, on whose computer system the information is stored or hosted or published, upon obtaining knowledge by itself or been brought to actual knowledge by an affected person in writing or through email signed with electronic signature about any such information should act within thirty six hours and where applicable, work with user or owner of such information to disable such information. Further the intermediary should preserve such information and associated records for at least ninety days for investigation purposes.

- The Intermediary should inform its users that in case of non-compliance with rules and regulations, user agreement and privacy policy for access or usage of intermediary computer resource, the Intermediary has the right to immediately terminate the access or usage lights of the users to the computer resource of Intermediary and remove non-compliant information.

- The intermediary should strictly follow the provisions of the Act or any other laws for the time being in force.

When required by lawful order, the intermediary should provide information or any such assistance to Government Agencies who are lawfully authorised for investigative, protective, cyber security activity.

- The intermediary should take all reasonable measures to secure its computer resource and information contained therein.

- The intermediary should report cyber security incidents and also share cyber security incidents related information with the Indian Computer Emergency Response Team.

- The intermediary should not knowingly deploy or install or modify the technical configuration of computer resource or become party to any such act which may change or has the potential to change the normal course of operation of the computer resource than what it is supposed to "perform thereby circumventing any law for the time being in force.

- The intermediary should publish on its website the name of the Grievance Officer and his contact details as well as mechanism by which users or any victim who suffers as a result of access or usage of computer resource by any person can notify their complaints against such access or usage of computer resource of the intermediary or other matters pertaining to the computer resources made available by it. The Grievance Officer should redress the complaints within one month from the date of receipt of complaint.

RULES ISSUED UNDER THE IT ACT, 2000

The Information Technology (Reasonable security practices and procedures and sensitive personal data or information) Rules, 2011
These rules are regarding sensitive personal data or information and are applicable to the body corporate or any person located within India. It basically require entities holding sensitive personal information of users to maintain certain specified security standards.

The Information Technology (Electronic Service Delivery) Rules, 2011
These rules provide for creation of a system of electronic delivery of services. Under the Electronic Service Delivery Rules the government can specify certain services, such as applications, certificates, licenses etc, to be delivered electronically.

The Information Technology (Intermediaries guidelines) Rules, 2011
These rules provide the rights and responsibilities of internet intermediaries in India. If the Internet intermediaries follow these rules and exercise proper cyber due diligence, they are entitled to a "safe harbour protection". Otherwise, they are liable for various acts or omission occurring at their respective platforms once the matter has been brought to their notice.

The Information Technology (Guidelines for Cyber Cafe) Rules, 2011
According to these guidelines, cyber cafes should register themselves with an appropriate government agency, and provide services to users only after establishing their identity. It also deals with maintenance of records of such identity as well as log of sites visited, among others.

The Cyber Appellate Tribunal (Salary, Allowances and other terms and conditions of service of Chairperson and Members) Rules, 2009
These rules provide for the salary, allowances and terms of service of the Chairperson and members of the Cyber Appellate Tribunal.

The Cyber Appellate Tribunal (Procedure for investigation of Misbehaviour or Incapacity of Chairperson and Members) Rules, 2009
These rules provide for the procedure for investigation of misbehavior or incapacity of the Chairperson and members of the Cyber Appellate Tribunal.

The Information Technology (Procedure and Safeguards for Blocking for Access of Information by Public), 2009
The rules provide for the designation of an officer of the Central Government for the purpose of issuing direction for blocking for access by the public any information generated, transmitted, received, stored or hosted in any computer resource. It provides the procedure and the safeguards to be followed by the designated officer.

The Information Technology (Procedure and Safeguards for interception, monitoring and decryption of information) Rules, 2009
These rules explain the procedure and safeguards subject to which such interception or monitoring or decryption may be carried out.

The Information Technology (Procedure and Safeguard for Monitoring and Collecting Traffic Data or

Information) Rules, 2009

It contains the procedure for aggregate monitoring of communications and the procedural safeguards to be observed in them.

The Information Technology (Use of electronic records and digital signatures) Rules, 2004
These rules deal with the manner and format in which the electronic records should be filed, created or issued. It also states the manner or method of payment of any fees or charges for filing or creating any electronic record.

The Information Technology (Security Procedure) Rules, 2004
These rules prescribe the provisions relating to secure digital signatures and secure electronic records.

The Information Technology (Other Standards) Rules, 2003
The rules deal with the standards to be observed by the Controller to ensure that the secrecy and security of the digital signatures are assured.

The Information Technology (Certifying Authority) Regulations, 2001
The regulation details the technical standards and procedures to be used by a Certifying Authority.

Information Technology (Certifying Authorities) Rules, 2000
This rule deals with licensing of Certifying authorities and the procedures that need to be complied by them. It also prescribed the eligibility, appointment and working of Certifying Authorities.

Information Technology (Amendment) Act, 2008

This IT Act 2000 was amended by Information Technology Amendment Bill, 2008 which was passed in Lok Sabha on 22nd December, 2008 and in Rajya Sabha on 23rd December, 2008. It received the assent of the President on 5th February 2009 and was notified with effect from 27/10/2009.

A major amendment was made in 2008. It introduced the Section 66A which penalized sending of "offensive messages". It also introduced the Section 69, which gave authorities the power of "interception or monitoring or decryption of any information through any computer resource". It also introduced for child porn, cyber terrorism and voyeurism. It was passed on 22 December 2008 without any debate in Lok Sabha. The next day it was passed by the Rajya Sabha. It was signed by the then President (Pratibha Patil) on 5 February 2009.

The new amendments to the Information Technology Act, 2000 that got passed by the Lok Sabha in December 2008, has number of positive developments, as well as many which dismay. Positively, they signal an attempt by the government to create a dynamic policy that is technology neutral. This is exemplified by its embracing the idea of electronic signatures as opposed to digital signatures. But more could have been done on this front (for instance, section 76 of the Act still talks of floppy disks). There have also been attempts to deal proactively with the many new challenges that the Internet poses.

Freedom of Expression

The first amongst these challenges is that of child pornography. It is heartening to see that the section on child pornography (s.67B) has been drafted with some degree of care. It talks only of sexualized representations of actual children, and does not include fantasy play-acting by adults, etc. From a plain reading of the section, it is unclear whether drawings depicting children will also be deemed an offence under the section. Unfortunately, the section covers everyone who performs the conducts outlined in the section, including minors. A slight awkwardness is created by the age of "children" being defined in the explanation to section 67B as older than the age of sexual consent. So a person who is capable of having sex legally may not record such activity (even for private purposes) until he or she turns eighteen.

Another problem is that the word "transmit" has only been defined for section 66E. The phrase "causes to be transmitted" is used in section 67, 67A, and 67B. That phrase, on the face of it, would include the recipient who initiates a transmission along with the person from whose server the data is sent. While in India, traditionally the person charged with obscenity is the person who produces and distributes the obscene material, and not the consumer of such material.

This new amendment might prove to be a change in that position.
Section 66A which punishes persons for sending offensive messages is overly broad, and is patently in violation of Art. 19(1)(a) of our Constitution. The fact that some information is "grossly offensive" (s.66A(a)) or that it causes "annoyance" or "inconvenience" while being known to be false (s.66A(c)) cannot be a reasons for curbing the freedom of speech unless it is directly related to decency or morality, public order, or defamation (or any of the four other grounds listed in Art. 19(2)). It must be stated here that many argue that John Stuart Mill's harm principle provides a better framework for freedom of expression than Joel Feinberg's offence principle. The latter part of s.66A(c), which talks of deception, is sufficient to combat spam and phishing, and hence the first half, talking of annoyance or inconvenience is not required. Additionally, it would be beneficial if an explanation could be added to s.66A(c) to make clear what "origin" means in that section. Because depending on the construction of that word s.66A(c) can, for instance, unintentionally prevent organisations from using proxy servers, and may prevent a person from using a sender envelope different form the "from" address in an e-mail (a feature that many e-mail providers like Gmail implement to allow people to send mails from their work account while being logged in to their personal account). Furthermore, it may also prevent remailers, tunnelling, and other forms of ensuring anonymity online. This doesn't seem to be what is intended by the legislature, but the section might end up having that effect. This should hence be clarified.

Section 69A grants powers to the Central Government to "issue directions for blocking of public access to any information through any computer resource". In English, that would mean that it allows the government to block any website. While necessity or expediency in terms of certain restricted interests are specified, no guidelines have been specified. Those guidelines, per s.69A(2), "shall be such as may be prescribed". It has to be ensured that they are prescribed first, before any powers of censorship are granted to any body. In India, it is clear that any law that gives unguided discretion on an administrative authority to exercise censorship is unreasonable (In re Venugopal, AIR 1954 Mad 901).

Intermediary Liability
The amendment to the provision on intermediary liability (s.79) while a change in the positive direction, as is seeks to make only the actual violators of the law liable for the offences committed, still isn't wide enough. This exemption is required to be widely worded to encourage innovation and to allow for corporate and public initiatives for sharing of content, including via peer-to-peer technologies.

Firstly, the requirement of taking down content upon receiving "actual knowledge" is much too heavy a burden for intermediaries. Such a requirement forces the intermediary to make decisions rather than the appropriate authority (which often is the judiciary). The intermediary is no position to decide whether a Gauguin painting of Tahitian women is obscene or not, since that requires judicial application of mind. Secondly, that requirement is vitiates the principles of natural justice and freedom of expression because it allows a communication and news medium to be gagged without giving it, or the party communicating through it, any due hearing. It has been held by our courts that a restriction that does not provide the affected persons a right to be heard is procedurally unreasonable (Virendra v. State of Punjab, AIR 1957 SC 896).

The intermediary loses protection of the act if (a) it initiates the transmission; (b) selects the receiver of the transmission; and (c) selects or modifies the information. While the first two are required to be classified as true "intermediaries", the third requirement is a bit too widely worded. For instance, an intermediary might automatically inject advertisements in all transmissions, but that modification does not go to the heart of the transmission, or make it responsible for the transmission in any way. Similarly, the intermediary may have a code of conduct, and may regulate transmissions with regard to explicit language (which is easy to judge), but would not have the capability to make judgments regarding fair use of copyrighted materials. So that kind of "selection" should not render the intermediary liable, since misuse of copyright might well be against the intermediary's terms and conditions of use.

Privacy and Surveillance
While the threat of cyber-terrorism might be very real, blanket monitoring of traffic is not the way forward to get results, and is sure to prove counter-productive. It is much easy to find a needle in a small bale of hay rather than in a haystack. Thus, it must be ensured that until the procedures and safeguards mentioned in sub-sections 69(2) and 69B(2) are drafted before the powers granted by those sections are exercised. Small-scale and targetted monitoring of metadata (called "traffic data" in the Bill) is a much more suitable solution, that will actually lead to results, instead of getting information overload through unchannelled monitoring of large quantities of data. If such safeguards aren't in place, then the powers might be of suspect constitutionality because of lack of guided exercise of those powers.

Very importantly, the government must also follow up on these powers by being transparent about the kinds of monitoring that it does to ensure that the civil and human rights guaranteed by our Constitution are upheld at all times.

Encryption
The amending bill does not really bring about much of a change with respect to encryption, except for expanding the scope of the government's power to order decryption. While earlier, under section 69, the Controller had powers to order decryption for certain purposes and order 'subscribers' to aid in doing so (with a sentence of up to seven years upon non-compliance), now the government may even call upon intermediaries to help it with decryption (s.69(3)). Additionally, s.118 of the Indian Penal Code has been amended to recognize the use of encryption as a possible means of concealment of a 'design to commit [an] offence punishable with death or imprisonment for life'.

The government already controls the strength of permissible encryption by way of the Internet Service Provider licences, and now has explicitly been granted the power to do so by s.84A of the Act. However, the government may only prescribe the modes or methods of encryption "for secure use of the electronic medium and for promotion of e-governance and e-commerce". Thus, it is possible to read that as effectively rendering nugatory the government's efforts to restrict the strength of encryption to 40-bit keys (for symmetric encryption).
Other Penal Provisions

Section 66F(1)(B), defining "cyberterrorism" is much too wide, and includes unauthorised access to information on a computer with a belief that that information may be used to cause injury to decency or morality or defamation, even. While there is no one globally accepted definition of cyberterrorism, it is tough to conceive of slander as a terrorist activity.

Another overly broad provision is s.43, which talks of "diminish[ing] its value or utility" while referring information residing on a computer, is overly broad and is not guided by the statute. Diminishing of the value of information residing on a computer could be done by a number of different acts, even copying of unpublished data by a conscientious whistleblower might, for instance, fall under this clause. While the statutory interpretation principle of noscitur a socii (that the word must be understood by the company it keeps) might be sought to be applied, in this case that doesn't give much direction either.

While all offences carrying penalties above three years imprisonment have been made cognizable, they have also been made bailable and lesser offences have been made compoundable. This is a desirable amendment, especially given the very realistic possibility of incorrect imprisonments (Airtel case, for instance), and frivolous cases that are being registered (Orkut obscenity cases).

Cheating by personation is not defined, and it is not clear whether it refers to cheating as referred to under the Indian Penal Code as conducted by communication devices, or whether it is creating a new category of offence. In the latter case, it is not at all clear whether a restricted meaning will be given to those words by the court such that only cases of phishing are penalised, or whether other forms of anonymous communications or other kinds of disputes in virtual worlds (like Second Life) will be brought under the meaning of "personation" and "cheating".

While it must be remembered that more law is not always an answer to dealing with problems, whether online or otherwise, it is good to note that the government has sought to address the newer problems that have arisen due to newer technologies. But equally important is the requirement to train both the judiciary and the law enforcement personnel to minimize the possibility of innocent citizens being harassed.

Features of the Information Technology (Amendment) Act, 2008
        The term 'digital signature' has been replaced with 'electronic signature' to make the Act more technology neutral.

        A new section has been inserted to define 'communication device' to mean cell phones, personal digital assistance or combination of both or any other device used to communicate, send or transmit any text video, audio or image.

        A new section has been added to define cyber cafe as any facility from where the access to the internet is offered by any person in the ordinary course of business to the members of the public.

        A new definition has been inserted for intermediary.

        A new section 10A has been inserted to the effect that contracts concluded electronically shall not be deemed to be unenforceable solely on the ground that electronic form or means was used.

        The damages of Rs. One Crore prescribed under section 43 of the earlier Act of 2000 for damage to computer, computer system etc. has been deleted and the relevant parts of the section have been substituted by the words, 'he shall be liable to pay damages by way of compensation to the person so affected'.

        A new section 43A has been inserted to protect sensitive personal data or information possessed, dealt or handled by a body corporate in a computer resource which such body corporate owns, controls or operates. If such body corporate is negligent in implementing and maintaining reasonable security practices and procedures and thereby causes wrongful loss or wrongful gain to any person, it shall be liable to pay damages by way of compensation to the person so affected.

        Sections 66A to 66F has been added to Section 66 prescribing punishment for offences such as obscene electronic message transmissions, identity theft, cheating by impersonation using computer resource, violation of privacy and cyber terrorism.

        Section 67 of the IT Act, 2000 has been amended to reduce the term of imprisonment for publishing or transmitting obscene material in electronic form to three years from five years and increase the fine thereof from Rs.100,000 to Rs. 500,000. Sections 67A to 67C have also been inserted. While Sections 67A and B deals with penal provisions in respect of offences of publishing or transmitting material containing sexually explicit act and child pornography in electronic form, Section 67C deals with the obligation of an intermediary to preserve and retain such information as may be specified for such duration and in such manner and format as the central government may prescribe.

In view of the increasing threat of terrorism in the country, the new amendments include an amended section 69 giving power to the state to issue directions for interception or monitoring of decryption of any information through any computer resource.

Further, sections 69A and B, two new sections, grant power to the state to issue directions for blocking for public access of any information through any computer resource and to authorize to monitor and collect traffic data or information through any computer resource for cyber security.

Section 79 of the Act which exempted intermediaries has been modified to the effect that an intermediary shall not be liable for any third party information data or communication link made available or hosted by him if; (a) The function of the intermediary is limited to providing access to a communication system over which information made available by third parties is transmitted or temporarily stored or hosted; (b) The intermediary does not initiate the transmission or select the receiver of the transmission and select or modify the information contained in the transmission; (c)

The intermediary observes due diligence while discharging his duties. However, section 79 will not apply to an intermediary if the intermediary has conspired or abetted or aided or induced whether by threats or promise or otherwise in the commission of the unlawful act or upon receiving actual knowledge or on being notified that any information, data or communication link residing in or connected to a computer resource controlled by it is being used to commit an unlawful act, the intermediary fails to expeditiously remove or disable access to that material on that resource without vitiating the evidence in any manner.

A proviso has been added to Section 81 which states that the provisions of the Act shall have overriding effect. The proviso states that nothing contained in the Act shall restrict any person from exercising any right conferred under the Copyright Act, 1957.

National Policy on Information Technology 2012

The Union Cabinet has recently in September 2012, approved the National Policy on Information Technology 2012. The Policy aims to leverage Information & Communication Technology (ICT) to address the country's economic and developmental challenges.

The vision of the Policy is "To strengthen and enhance India's position as the Global IT hub and to use IT and cyber space as an engine for rapid, inclusive and substantial growth in the national economy". The Policy envisages among other objectives, to increase revenues of IT and ITES Industry from 100 Billion USD at present to 300 Billion USD by 2020 and expand exports from 69 Billion USD at present to 200 Billion USD by 2020. It also aims to create a pool of 10 million additional skilled manpower in ICT.

The thrust areas of the policy include:

To increase revenues of IT and ITES (Information Technology Enabled Services) Industry from 100 Billion USD currently to 300 Billion USD by 2020 and expand exports from 69 Billion USD currently to 200 Billion USD by 2020.

To gain significant global market-share in emerging technologies and Services.

To promote innovation and R&D in cutting edge technologies and development of applications and solutions in areas like localization, location based services, mobile value added services, Cloud Computing, Social Media and Utility models.

To encourage adoption of ICTs in key economic and strategic sectors to improve their competitiveness and productivity.

To provide fiscal benefits to SMEs and Startups for adoption of IT in value creation

To create a pool of 10 million additional skilled manpower in ICT.

To make at least one individual in every household e-literate.

To provide for mandatory delivery of and affordable access to all public services in electronic mode.

To enhance transparency, accountability, efficiency, reliability and decentralization in Government and in particular, in delivery of public services.

To leverage ICT for key Social Sector initiatives like Education, Health, Rural Development and Financial Services to promote equity and quality.

To make India the global hub for development of language technologies, to encourage and facilitate development of content accessible in all Indian languages and thereby help bridge the digital divide.

To enable access of content and ICT applications by differently-abled people to foster inclusive development.

To leverage ICT for expanding the workforce and enabling life-long learning.

To strengthen the Regulatory and Security Framework for ensuring a Secure and legally compliant Cyberspace ecosystem.

To adopt Open standards and promote open source and open technologies The Policy has however not yet been notified in the Official Gazette.

Information Technology (Amendment) Bill, 2015

On 2 April 2015, the Chief Minister of Maharashtra, Devendra Fadnavis revealed to the state assembly that a new law was being framed to replace the repealed Section 66A. Fadnavis was replying to a query Shiv Sena leader Neelam Gorhe. Gorhe had said that repeal of the law would encourage online miscreants and asked whether the state government would frame a law to this regard. Fadnavis said that the previous law had resulted in no convictions, so the law would be framed such that it would be strong and result in convictions.[33]

On 13 April 2015, it announced that the Ministry of Home Affairs would form a committee of officials from the Intelligence Bureau, Central Bureau of Investigation, National Investigation Agency, Delhi Police and ministry itself to produce a new legal framework. This step was reportedly taken after complaints from intelligence agencies that, they were no longer able to counter online posts that involved national security matter or incite people to commit an offence, such as online recruitment for ISIS.[34][35] Former Minister of State with the Ministry of Information Technology, Milind Deora has supported a new "unambiguous section to replace 66A"

Bill No. 57 of 2015
THE INFORMATION TECHNOLOGY (AMENDMENT) BILL, 2015
By
SHRI JAGDAMBIKA PAL, M.P.
A
BILL

further to amend the Information Technology Act, 2000.

BE it enacted by Parliament in the Sixty-sixth Year of the Republic of India as follows:—

1.
(1) This Act may be called the Information Technology (Amendment) Act, 2015.Short title and commencement.
(2) It shall come into force at once.

2. In the information Technology Act, 2000, in section 66A,
(i) clause (a) shall be omitted;
(ii) in clause (b), the words "annoyance, inconvenience," shall be omitted;
(iii) in clause (c), the words "for the purpose of causing annoyance or inconvenience or" shall be omitted; and
(iv) after clause (c), for the words "three years and with fine" the words "one month or with fine" shall be substituted.

STATEMENT OF OBJECTS AND REASONS

Right to Freedom of Speech and Expression is a fundamental principal for any vibrant democracy. The founding fathers of Indian constitution undoubtedly considered free speech as one of the most basic rights, essential for safeguarding and promoting other human rights. While providing for Right to free speech under article 19(1)(a) of the Constitution, certain reasonable restrictions under article 19(2) have been laid down. Therefore, free speech can be restricted only on the grounds of reasonable restrictions as mentioned in article 19(2). Section 66A of the Information Technology Act, 2000 in its current form is arbitrary and does not adhere to the standards laid down by article 19(2) and the interpretation yardsticks laid down by the Hon'ble Supreme Court.

The phrases used in section 66A such as causing inconvenience, is of menacing character and vague and have a tendency of being used arbitrarily, leading to chilling effects on free speech and other rights of the citizens. It provides for criminal recourse for speech that is grossly offensive and aims at merely causing "annoyance" or "inconvenience". These phrases are very subjective and vague and not in conformity with the restrictions mentioned under article 19(2) and thus create new offences hampering the online right to freedom of expression.

In the last few years, there have been several instances of misuse of this provision such as the arrests of cartoonists, university professors for posting caricatures for criticizing the Government's ineffectiveness and even the arrest of teenagers for questioning shutdown of a city on social networks like Facebook. These arbitrary arrests highlight the potential abuse of this provision due to the subjective powers conferred on the police.

Moreover, section 127 of the United Kingdom Communications Act, 2003, from which the phraseology of section 66A has been borrowed was also struck down by the House of Lords in the case of Director of

Public Prosecutions vs. Collins. It was held that Parliament could not have intended to criminalize statements that one person may reasonably find to be polite and acceptable and another may decide to be grossly offensive. However, section 66A continues to provide punishment without any safeguard or judicially evolved checks and balances guiding the interpretation regarding the ingredients of the offence warranting invoking of the provision.

Section 66A of Information Technology Act provides punishment up to three years of imprisonment and fine without any upper limit. The punishment prima-facie is disproportional to the offence mentioned. There is no reasonable justification provided as to why punishment for sending offensive messages through communication service should extend to three years with a fine, particularly when the punishment for criminal nuisance under the Indian Penal Code, 1860 extends to a fine of rupees two thousand with no imprisonment. It is not surprising that due to such provisions, India was ranked at 140th place out of 179 countries in the Press Freedom Index, 2013. Therefore, the provisions in its current form is violative of several human rights and in direct contravention of the principle of right to free speech and expression and need to be amended.

Hence this Bill.

NEW DELHI;   JAGDAMBIKA PAL

February 12, 2015

ANNEXURE

EXTRACT FROM THE INFORMATION TECHNOLOGY, 2000

(21 OF 2000)

66A. Any person who sends, by means of a computer resource or a communication device,—

(a) any information that is grossly offensive or has menacing character; or

(b) any information which he knows to be false, but for the purpose of causing annoyance, inconvenience, danger, obstruction, insult, injury, criminal intimidation,, enmity, hatred or ill will, persistently by making use of such computer resource or a communication device; or

(c) any electronic mail or electronic mail message for the purpose of causing annoyance or inconvenience or to deceive or to mislead the addressee or recipient about the origin of such messages,

shall be punishable with imprisonment for a term which may extend to three years and with fine.

LOK SABHA
A
BILL
further to amend the Information Technology Act, 2000.
(Shri Jagdambika Pal, M.P.)
GMGIPMRND—4746LS(S3)—03-03-2015.

5

ELECTRONIC COMMERCE & IT Act 2000

Electronic commerce, commonly known as e-commerce or e-comm, is the buying and selling of products or services over electronic systems such as the Internet and other computer networks. Electronic commerce draws on such technologies as electronic funds transfer, supply chain management, Internet marketing, online transaction processing, electronic data interchange (EDI), inventory management systems, and automated data collection systems. Modern electronic commerce typically uses the World Wide Web (www) at least at one point in the transaction's life-cycle, although it may encompass a wider range of technologies such as e-mail, mobile devices and telephones as well.

Contemporary electronic commerce involves everything from ordering "digital" content for immediate online consumption, to ordering conventional goods and services, to "meta" services to facilitate other types of electronic commerce.

On the institutional level, big corporations and financial institutions use the internet to exchange financial data to facilitate domestic and international business. Data integrity and security are very hot and pressing issues for electronic commerce.

E-commerce can be divided into:

> E-tailing or "virtual storefronts" on Web sites with online catalogs, sometimes gathered into a "virtual mall".

> The gathering and use of demographic data through Web contacts.

> Electronic Data Interchange (EDI), the business-to-business exchange of data.
> E-mail and fax and their use as media for reaching prospects and established customers (for example, with newsletters).

> Business-to-business buying and selling.

> The security of business transactions.

E-commerce in India

India has an internet user base of over 100 million users. The penetration of e-commerce is low compared to markets like the United States and the United Kingdom but is growing at a much faster rate with a large number of new entrants.

The industry consensus is that growth is at an inflection point with key drivers being:

- Increasing broadband Internet and 3Gpenetration.

- Rising standards of living and a burgeoning, upwardly mobile middle class with high disposable incomes.

- Availability of much wider product range compared to what is available at brick and mortar retailers.

- Busy lifestyles, urban traffic congestion and lack of time for offline shopping.

- Lower prices compared to brick and mortar retail driven by disintermediation and reduced inventory and real estate costs.

- Increased usage of online classified sites, with more consumers buying and selling second-hand goods.

- Evolution of the online marketplace model with sites like ebay, Infibeam, and Tradus.

The India retail market is estimated at $470 Bn in 2011 and is expected to grow to $850 Bn by 2020, – estimated CAGR of 7%. According to Forrester, the e-commerce market in India is set to grow the fastest within the Asia-Pacific Region at a CAGR of over 57% between 2012-16. India e-tailing market in 2011 was about $600 Mn and expected to touch $70 Bn by 2020 – estimated CAGR of 61%. The Online Travel Industry is the biggest segment in eCommerce and is booming largely due to the Internet-savvy urban population.

Some of the aspects of Indian e-commerce that are unique to India (and potentially to other developing countries) are:

- Cash on Delivery as a preferred payment method. India has a vibrant cash economy as a result of which 80% of Indian e-commerce tends to be Cash on Delivery (COD).

- Direct Imports constitute a large component of online sales. Demand for international consumer products is growing much faster than in-country supply from authorized distributors and e-commerce offerings.

E-commerce websites are Internet intermediaries within the meaning of IT Act, 2000. "Intermediary" with respect to any particular electronic records, means any person who on behalf of another person receives, stores or transmits that record or provides any service with respect to that record and includes telecom service providers, network service providers, internet service providers, web hosting service providers, search engines, online payment sites, online-auction sites, online market places and cyber cafes. The IT (Intermediaries Guidelines) Rules of 2011 regulate the functioning of e-commerce websites. Cyber law due diligence is the main aspect that all e-commerce site owners should comply with.

ELECTRONIC CONTRACTS

E-Contracts are conceptually very similar to the traditional paper-based Commercial Contracts.

Electronic contracts (contracts that are not paper based but rather in electronic form) are born out of the need for speed, convenience and efficiency.

In the electronic age, the whole transaction can be completed in seconds, with both parties simply affixing their digital signatures to an electronic copy of the contract. There is no need for delayed couriers and additional travelling costs in such a scenario. The conventional law relating to contracts i.e. The Indian Contract Act of 1872 is not sufficient to address all the issues that arise in electronic contracts. The Information Technology Act solves some of the peculiar issues that arise in the formation and authentication of electronic contracts.

An e-contract is a contract modelled, executed and enacted by a software system. Computer programs are used to automate business processes that govern e-contracts.

Like any other contract, an e-contract also require the following –

Offer to be made – The offer is not made by website displaying the items for sale at a particular price. This is actually an invitation to offer and hence is revocable at any time up to the time of acceptance. The offer is made by the customer on placing the products in the virtual 'basket' or 'shopping cart' for payment.

Offer to be accepted – The acceptance is usually undertaken by the business after the offer has been made by the consumer in relation with the invitation to offer. Offers and acceptances can be exchanged entirely by e-mail; the seller can offer goods or services (e.g. air tickets, software etc) through his website; users may need to accept an online agreement in order to be able to avail of the services.

Lawful consideration – Contract to be enforceable by law must have lawful consideration, i.e., when both parties give and receive something in return.

Intention to create legal relations
Parties must be competent to contract
There must be free and genuine consent
Object of the contract must be lawful

There must be certainty and possibility of performance

Chapter IV of the Information Technology Act, 2000 i.e. sections 11, 12 and 13 covers the aspects of Attribution, Acknowledgment and Despatch of Electronic Records.

According to Sec.10A of the IT Act, 2000, a communication or contract shouldn't be denied or declared void merely because it's in electronic form. It thereby acknowledges the legal validity of e-contracts.

6

CYBER FRAUDS

The Internet has become a basic fact of everyday life for millions of people worldwide, from e-mail to online shopping. Ever faster and more accessible connections available on a wider range of platforms, such as mobile phones or person to person portable devices, have spurred new e-commerce opportunities. Online shopping and banking are increasingly widespread and over the next 10 years, the Net is expected to become as common as gas or electricity. The invention of the computers has opened new avenues for the fraudsters. It is an evil having its origin in the growing dependence on computers in modern life.

Fraud is the intentional deception of a person or group for the purpose of stealing property or money. Internet fraud includes any scheme using Web sites, chat rooms, and email to offer nonexistent goods and services to consumers or to communicate false information to consumers. Customers then pay for the fraudulent goods over the Internet with their credit cards. Internet fraud involves a wide variety of schemes limited only by the imagination and creativity of a seller intent on deceiving a buyer. A few general characteristics one can find in all cyber scams. Most scams are done by e-mail. They entice users to give them critical information like usernames, passwords, credit card information, or other types of account information.

Cyber fraud has the potential of hindering the economic and social development of any nation. This is because among other dire consequences, foreign investment is seriously discouraged. Cyber fraud can also destroy our good and morally sound culture. This is because the youth will no longer work but resort to that means to earn their living.

Types of cyber frauds
A wide variety of scams operate in the online environment, ranging from fraudulent lottery schemes, travel and credit-related ploys, modem and web page hijacking, and identity theft (ID theft) to name but a few. Many of these scams, such as pyramid selling, are simply online variants of fraudulent practices that have long existed offline. However, the Internet has given criminals access to a worldwide base of consumer targets as well as more opportunities to elude enforcement as they need not be in the same country, or even in the same hemisphere, as their victims.

The Internet allows fraudsters to masquerade as legitimate traders behind professional-looking websites or on virtual auction sites to advertise "free" or "bargain" prices, "miracle" products, and "exciting" investment and business opportunities. These deceptive and misleading offers trick unsuspecting consumers into buying goods and services on line which turn out to be far less than promised or even non-existent.

Many online scams originate in spam messages – usually through e-mail, but sometimes through text messages (SMS), voice messages delivered by Internet (Voice-over Internet Protocol or – VoIP) or other electronic channels. Spam has evolved into a vehicle for the spread of fraud and other online abuses. Many e-mail users will have received a message from a person claiming to be a government official or member of the royal family of a foreign country (usually in Africa), promising substantial sums of money in return for assistance in transferring money out of the country. Commonly known as the "Nigerian", "West African" or "419" scam, once it has sucked in victims it convinces them to make small advance payments for various reasons, such as banking transaction fees. Needless to say, the victim never receives the promised substantial sums in return. Many pyramid and work-at-home schemes are also distributed through spam and follow the "advance fee fraud" format of requiring up-front payment or investment on the promise of high returns that are never forthcoming.

Spam is a key tool for the spread of ID theft, luring people into disclosing sensitive information such as credit card numbers or passwords. For example, phishing spams falsely claim to come from legitimate and well-known financial institutions or merchants. They ask recipients to click through on hyperlinks in order to verify or update their online accounts. These hyperlinks direct users to fake "look alike" websites where users are tricked into divulging personal information which can be used to access and illegally transfer money out of the victim's bank account(s), open new bank or credit card accounts in the victim's name, make unlawful online purchases, etc.

These attacks are continually becoming more sophisticated. The past year has seen the growth of a new practice known as spear-phishing where accurate information about the recipient, such as the full name and home address, is included in the phishing e-mail making it even more convincing. Another new phenomenon known as vishing tricks people into making phone calls rather than clicking on links to websites. The number given is to a VoIP phone which records digits (such as account numbers) entered into the telephone, again enabling crooks to steal and use the information.

Other variants of fraud rely on the use of identity stolen through technological methods. For example, pharming interferes with the domain name system

(DNS) look up process and redirects users attempting to reach a particular website to a "spoofed" one where they divulge personal information to the crooks. Malware (or malicious software), can be downloaded unwittingly by consumers from spam attachments or as they surf on line. Such malicious code, which increasingly targets mobile phones and other portable devices in addition to computers, can install "key stroke" loggers and other programs to steal information stored on, entered into, or received by these devices. The information collected through these kinds of technological attacks, such as passwords and other sensitive data, can then be used to perpetrate fraud.

Cyber frauds in India
According to Norton Cybercrime Report 2012, 66% of Indian online adults have been a victim of cyber fraud in their lifetime. In the past 12 months, 56% of online adults in India have experienced cyber fraud.

As per the report, at least 1,15,000 people fall prey to cyber fraud every day, while 80 per minute and more than one per second leading to a rise in the average direct financial cost per victim to around Rs10,500.

According to the survey, the cybercriminals have now shifted their focus to the increasingly popular social platforms. One in three adults online Indians (32%) have been either social or mobile cybercrime victims. While most internet users delete suspicious emails and are careful with their personal details online. However, 25% don't use complex passwords or change their passwords frequently and 38% do not check for the padlock symbol in the browser before entering sensitive personal information.

Online adults are also unaware of the evolution of most common forms of cybercrime. In fact, 68% of adults do not know that malware can operate in a discreet fashion, making it hard to know if a computer has been compromised, and one third (35%) are not certain that their computer is currently clean and free of viruses.

Types Cyber Crimes In India
Some types of cyber crimes found in India are:

1. Cyber pornography
This would include pornographic websites; pornographic magazines produced using computers (to publish and print the material) and the Internet (to download and transmit pornographic pictures, photos, writings etc). (Delhi Public School case)

2. Sale of illegal articles
This would include sale of narcotics, weapons and wildlife etc., by posting information on websites, auction websites, and bulletin boards or simply by using email communication. E.g. many of the auction sites even in India are believed to be selling cocaine in the name of 'honey'.

3. Online gambling
There are millions of websites; all hosted on servers abroad, that offer online gambling. In fact, it is believed that many of these websites are actually fronts for money laundering. Cases of hawala transactions and money laundering over the Internet have been reported. Whether these sites have any relationship with drug trafficking is yet to be explored.

Recent Indian case about cyber lotto was very interesting. A man called Kola Mohan invented the story of winning the Euro Lottery. He himself created a website and an email address on the Internet with the address

'eurolottery@usa.net.' Whenever accessed, the site would name him as the beneficiary of the 12.5 million pound. After confirmation a Telugu newspaper published this as a news. He collected huge sums from the public as well as from some banks for mobilization of the deposits in foreign currency. However, the fraud came to light when a cheque discounted by him with the Andhra Bank for Rs 1.73 million bounced.

Mohan had pledged with Andhra Bank the copy of a bond certificate purportedly issued by Midland Bank, Sheffields, London stating that a term deposit of 12.5 million was held in his name.

4. Intellectual Property crimes
These include software piracy, copyright infringement, trademarks violations, theft of computer source code etc. In other words this is also referred to as cyber squatting. Satyam Vs. Siffy is the most widely known case. Bharti Cellular Ltd. filed a case in the Delhi High Court that some cyber squatters had registered domain names such as barticellular.com and bhartimobile.com with Network solutions under different fictitious names. The court directed Network Solutions not to transfer the domain names in question to any third party and the matter is sub-judice. Similar issues had risen before various High Courts earlier. Yahoo had sued one Akash Arora for use of the domain name 'Yahooindia.Com' deceptively similar to its 'Yahoo.com'. As this case was governed by the

Trade Marks Act, 1958, the additional defence taken against Yahoo's legal action for the interim order was that the Trade Marks Act was applicable only to goods.

5. Email spoofing
A spoofed email is one that appears to originate from one source but actually has been sent from another source. E.g. Gauri has an e-mail address gauri@indiaforensic.com. Her enemy, Prasad spoofs her e-mail and sends obscene messages to all her acquaintances. Since the e-mails appear to have originated from Gauri, her friends could take offence and relationships could be spoiled for life.

Email spoofing can also cause monetary damage. In an American case, a teenager made millions of dollars by spreading false information about certain companies whose shares he had short sold. This misinformation was spread by sending spoofed emails, purportedly from news agencies like Reuters, to share brokers and investors who were informed that the companies were doing very badly. Even after the truth came out the values of the shares did not go back to the earlier levels and thousands of investors lost a lot of money.

Recently, a branch of the Global Trust Bank experienced a run on the bank. Numerous customers decided to withdraw all their money and close their accounts. It was revealed that someone had sent out spoofed emails to many of the bank's customers stating that the bank was in very bad shape financially and could close operations at any time. Unfortunately this information proved to be true in the next few days.

But the best example of the email spoofing can be given by an

Executive's case, where he pretended to be a girl and cheated an Abu dhabi based NRI for crores by blackmailing tactics.

6. Forgery
Counterfeit currency notes, postage and revenue stamps, mark sheets etc can be forged using sophisticated computers, printers and scanners. Outside many colleges across India, one finds touts soliciting the sale of fake mark sheets or even certificates. These are made using computers and high quality scanners and printers. In fact, this has becoming a booming business involving thousands of Rupees being given to student gangs in exchange for these bogus but authentic looking certificates. Some of the students are caught but this is very rare phenomenon.

7. Cyber Defamation
This occurs when defamation takes place with the help of computers and / or the Internet. E.g. someone publishes defamatory matter about someone on a website or sends e-mails containing defamatory information to all of that person's friends.
India's first case of cyber defamation was reported when a company's employee started sending derogatory, defamatory and obscene e-mails about its Managing Director. The e-mails were anonymous and frequent, and were sent to many of their business associates to tarnish the image and goodwill of the company.

The company was able to identify the employee with the help of a private computer expert and moved the Delhi High Court. The court granted an ad-interim injunction and restrained the employee from sending, publishing and transmitting e-mails, which are defamatory or derogatory to the plaintiffs.

8. Cyber stalking
The Oxford dictionary defines stalking as "pursuing stealthily". Cyber stalking involves following a person's movements across the Internet by posting message (sometimes threatening) on the bulletin boards frequented by the victim, entering the chat-rooms frequented by the victim, constantly bombarding the victim with emails etc.

9. Unauthorized access to computer systems or networks
This activity is commonly referred to as hacking. The Indian law has, however, given a different connotation to the term hacking, so we will not use the term "unauthorized access" interchangeably with the term "hacking". However, as per Indian law, unauthorized access does occur, if hacking has taken place. An active hackers' group, led by one "Dr. Nuker", who claims to be the founder of Pakistan Hackerz Club, reportedly hacked the websites of the Indian Parliament, Ahmedabad Telephone Exchange, Engineering Export Promotion Council, and United Nations (India).

10. Theft of information contained in electronic form

This includes information stored in computer hard disks, removable storage media etc.

11. Email bombing

Email bombing refers to sending a large number of emails to the victim resulting in the victim's email account (in case of an individual) or mail servers (in case of a company or an email service provider) crashing. In one case, a foreigner who had been residing in Simla, India for almost thirty years wanted to avail of a scheme introduced by the Simla Housing Board to buy land at lower rates. When he made an application it was rejected on the grounds that the scheme was available only for citizens of India. He decided to take his revenge. Consequently he sent thousands of mails to the Simla Housing Board and repeatedly kept sending e-mails till their servers crashed.

12. Data diddling

This kind of an attack involves altering raw data just before it is processed by a computer and then changing it back after the processing is completed. Electricity Boards in India have been victims to data diddling programs inserted when private parties were computerizing their systems. The NDMC Electricity Billing Fraud Case that took place in 1996 is a typical example. The computer network was used for receipt and accounting of electricity bills by the NDMC, Delhi. Collection of money, computerized accounting, record maintenance and remittance in his bank were exclusively left to a private contractor who was a computer professional. He misappropriated huge amount of funds by manipulating data files to show less receipt and bank remittance.

13. Salami attacks

These attacks are used for the commission of financial crimes. The key here is to make the alteration so insignificant that in a single case it would go completely unnoticed. E.g. a bank employee inserts a program, into the bank's servers, that deducts a small amount of money (say Rs. 5 a month) from the account of every customer. No account holder will probably notice this unauthorized debit, but the bank employee will make a sizeable amount of money every month.

To cite an example, an employee of a bank in USA was dismissed from his job. Disgruntled at having been supposedly mistreated by his employers the man first introduced a logic bomb into the bank's systems.

Logic bombs are programmes, which get activated on the occurrence of a particular predefined event. The logic bomb was programmed to take ten cents from all the accounts in the bank and put them into the account of the person whose name was alphabetically the last in the bank's rosters.

Then he went and opened an account in the name of Ziegler. The amount being withdrawn from each of the accounts in the bank was so insignificant that neither any of the account holders nor the bank officials noticed the fault.

It was brought to their notice when a person by the name of Zygler opened his account in that bank. He was surprised to find a sizeable amount of money being transferred into his account every Saturday.

Being an honest person, he reported the "mistake" to the bank authorities and the entire scheme was revealed.

14. Denial of Service attack

This involves flooding a computer resource with more requests than it can handle. This causes the resource (e.g. a web server) to crash thereby denying authorized users the service offered by the resource. Another variation to a typical denial of service attack is known as a Distributed Denial of Service (DDoS) attack wherein the perpetrators are many and are geographically widespread.

It is very difficult to control such attacks. The attack is initiated by sending excessive demands to the victim's computer(s), exceeding the limit that the victim's servers can support and making the servers crash.

Denial-of-service attacks have had an impressive history having, in the past, brought down websites like Amazon, CNN, Yahoo and eBay!

15. Virus / worm attacks

Viruses are programs that attach themselves to a computer or a file and then circulate themselves to other files and to other computers on a network. They usually affect the data on a computer, either by altering or deleting it. Worms, unlike viruses do not need the host to attach themselves to. They merely make functional copies of themselves and do this repeatedly till they eat up all the available space on a computer's memory.

The VBS_LOVELETTER virus (better known as the Love Bug or the ILOVEYOU virus) was reportedly written by a Filipino undergraduate. In May 2000, this deadly virus became the world's most prevalent virus. It struck one in every five personal computers in the world. When the virus was brought under check the true magnitude of the losses was incomprehensible. Losses incurred during this virus attack were pegged at US $ 10 billion. VBS_LOVELETTER utilized the addresses in Microsoft

Outlook and e-mailed itself to those addresses. The e-mail which was sent out had "ILOVEYOU" in its subject line. The attachment file was named "LOVE-LETTER-FOR-YOU.TXT.vbs". People wary of opening e-mail attachments were conquered by the subject line and those who had some knowledge of viruses, did not notice the tiny .vbs extension and believed the file to be a text file. The message in the e-mail was "kindly check the attached LOVELETTER coming from me".

Probably the world's most famous worm was the Internet worm let loose on the Internet by Robert Morris sometime in 1988. The Internet was, then, still in its developing years and this worm, which affected thousands of computers, almost brought its development to a complete halt. It took a team of experts almost three days to get rid of the worm and in the meantime many of the computers had to be disconnected from the network.

16. Logic bombs

These are event dependent programs. This implies that these programs are created to do something only when a certain event (known as a trigger event) occurs. E.g. even some viruses may be termed logic bombs because they lie dormant all through the year and become active only on a particular date (like the Chernobyl virus).

17. Trojan attacks

A Trojan as this program is aptly called is an unauthorized program which functions from inside what seems to be an authorized program, thereby concealing what it is actually doing. There are many simple ways of installing a Trojan in someone's computer. To cite an example, two friends Rahul and Mukesh (names changed), had a heated argument over one girl, Radha (name changed) whom they both liked. When the girl, asked to choose, chose Mukesh over Rahul, Rahul decided to get even. On the 14th of February, he sent Mukesh a spoofed e-card, which appeared to have come from Radha's mail account. The e-card actually contained a Trojan. As soon as Mukesh opened the card, the Trojan was installed on his computer. Rahul now had complete control over Mukesh's computer and proceeded to harass him thoroughly.

18. Internet time theft

This connotes the usage by an unauthorized person of the Internet hours paid for by another person. In May 2000, the economic offences wing, IPR section crime branch of Delhi police registered its first case involving theft of Internet hours. In this case, the accused, Mukesh Gupta an engineer with Nicom System (p) Ltd. was sent to the residence of the complainant to activate his Internet connection. However, the accused used Col. Bajwa's login name and password from various places causing wrongful loss of 100 hours to Col. Bajwa. Delhi police arrested the accused for theft of Internet time. On further inquiry in the case, it was found that Krishan Kumar, son of an ex army officer, working as senior executive in M/s Highpoint Tours & Travels had used Col Bajwa's login and passwords as many as 207 times from his residence and twice from his office. He confessed that Shashi Nagpal, from whom he had purchased a computer, gave the login and password to him. The police could not believe that time could be stolen. They were not aware of the concept of time-theft at all. Colonel Bajwa's report was rejected. He decided to approach The Times of India, New Delhi. They, in turn carried a report about the inadequacy of the New Delhi Police in handling cyber crimes. The Commissioner of Police, Delhi then took the case into his own hands and the police under his directions raided and arrested Krishan Kumar under sections 379, 411, 34 of IPC and section 25 of the Indian Telegraph Act. In another case, the Economic Offences Wing of

Delhi Police arrested a computer engineer who got hold of the password of an Internet user, accessed the computer and stole 107 hours of

Internet time from the other person's account. He was booked for the crime by a Delhi court during May 2000.

19. Web jacking
This occurs when someone forcefully takes control of a website (by cracking the password and later changing it). The actual owner of the website does not have any more control over what appears on that website. In a recent incident reported in the USA the owner of a hobby website for children received an e-mail informing her that a group of hackers had gained control over her website. They demanded a ransom of 1 million dollars from her. The owner, a schoolteacher, did not take the threat seriously. She felt that it was just a scare tactic and ignored the e-mail.

It was three days later that she came to know, following many telephone calls from all over the country, that the hackers had web jacked her website. Subsequently, they had altered a portion of the website which was entitled 'How to have fun with goldfish'. In all the places where it had been mentioned, they had replaced the word 'goldfish' with the word 'piranhas'. Piranhas are tiny but extremely dangerous flesh-eating fish.

Many children had visited the popular website and had believed what the contents of the website suggested. These unfortunate children followed the instructions, tried to play with piranhas, which they bought from pet shops, and were very seriously injured!

20. Theft of computer system
This type of offence involves the theft of a computer, some part(s) of a computer or a peripheral attached to the computer.

21. Physically damaging a computer system
This crime is committed by physically damaging a computer or its peripherals.

This is just a list of the known crimes in the cyber world. The unknown crimes might be far ahead of these, since the lawbreakers are always one-step ahead of lawmakers.

Who commits cyber crimes?
Insiders - Disgruntled employees and ex-employees, spouses, lovers
Hackers - Crack into networks with malicious intent
Virus Writers - Pose serious threats to networks and systems worldwide
Foreign Intelligence - Use cyber tools as part of their Services for espionage activities and can pose the biggest threat to the security of another country
Terrorists - Use to formulate plans, to raise funds, propaganda

How to Report Cyber crimes in India

Step 1- In case of any cybercrime, immediately approach the Law Enforcement Agency (LEA) i.e. Cyber Crime Bench or the nearest Police Station in your area. Here you can lodge FIR for commission of cybercrime under the relevant provisions of the Information Technology Act, 2000.

Step 2– The LEA then approaches the Indian Computer Response Team (CERT-in) for information pertaining to Technical Analysis of crime like IP address and URL details.

CERT-in- The CERT-In has been established under Section 70B of Information Technology (Amendment) Act 2008. The CERT-in has been conferred with the following functions in the area of cyber security:
*   Collection, analysis and dissemination of information on cyber incidents
*   Forecast and alerts of cyber security incidents
*   Emergency measures for handling cyber security incidents
*   Coordination of cyber incident response activities
*   Issue guidelines, advisories, vulnerability notes and whitepapers relating to information security practices, procedures, prevention, response and reporting of cyber incidents

Investigation of cyber crimes in India

In keeping with the demand of the times, the Cyber Crime Investigation Cell (CCIC) of the CBI, notified in September 1999, started functioning with effect from 3.3.2000. The Cell is headed by a Superintendent of Police. The jurisdiction of this Cell is all India, and besides the offences punishable under Chapter XI, IT Act, 2000, it also has power to look into other high-tech crimes. Cyber Crime Investigation Cell is a wing of Mumbai Police, India, to deal with Cyber crimes, and to enforce provisions of the Information Technology Act 2000, and various cyber crime related provisions of criminal laws, including the Indian Penal Code. Cyber Crime Investigation Cell is a part of Crime

Branch, Criminal Investigation Department of the Mumbai Police. The Cyber Crime Investigation Cell of Mumbai Police was inaugurated on 18th December 2000 and it is functioning under the overall guidance of Jt. Commissioner of Police (Crime), Addl. Commissioner of Police (Crime) and Dy. Commissioner of Police (Enforcement).

Cyber Crime Cells are also there at Delhi, Chennai, Bangalore, Hyderabad, Thane, Pune, Gujarat and Gurgaon.

The following information should be submitted while lodging a complaint -

1) **Victim of hacking** o

   Server Logs;

   Copy of defaced web page in soft copy as well as hard copy format, if website is defaced;

   If data is compromised on your server or computer or any other network equipment, soft copy of original data and soft copy of compromised data.

   Access control mechanism details i.e.- who had what kind of access to the compromised system;

   List of suspects – if the victim is having any suspicion on anyone.

   All relevant information leading to answers to the following questions –

   what ? (what is compromised)

   who? (who might have compromised system)

   when? (when the system was compromised)

   why? (why the system might have been compromised)

   where? (where is the impact of attack-identifying the target system from the network)

   How many? (How many systems have been compromised by the attack)

Victim of e-mail abuse, vulgar e-mail etc.

   Extract the extended headers of offending e-mail.

   o Bring soft copy as well hard copy of offending e-mail.

   o Please do not delete the offending e-mail from your e-mail box.

   Please save the copy of offending e-mail on your computer's hard drive.

Preventive Measures To Curb The Crime under Cyber Law India

Though by passage of time and improvement in technology to provide easier and user friendly methods to the consumer for make up their daily activities, it has lead to harsh world of security threats at the same time by agencies like hackers, crackers etc. various Information technology methods have introduced to curb such destructive activities to achieve the main objects of the technology to provide some sense of security to the users. Few basic prominent measures used to curb cyber crime are as follows:

Encryption

This however considered as an important tool for protecting data in transit. Plain text (readable) can thus converted to cipher text (coded language) by this method and the recipient of the data can decrypt it by converting it into plain text again by using private key. Except for recipient whose possessor of private key to decrypt the data, no one can gain access to sensitive information.

Not only the information in transit but also the information stored on computer can protected by using Conventional cryptography method. Usual problem lies during the distribution of keys as anyone if overhears it or intercept it can make the whole object of encryption to standstill. Public key encryptograpy was one solution to this where the public key could known to the whole world but the private key was only known to receiver, its very difficult to derive private key from public key.

Syncronised Passwords
These passwords are schemes used to change the password at user's and host token. The password on synchronised card changes every 30-60 seconds which only makes it valid for one time log-on session. Other useful methods introduced are signature, voice, fingerprint identification or retinal and biometric recognition etc. to impute passwords and pass phrases.

Firewalls
It creates wall between the system and possible intruders to protect the classified documents from leaked or accessed. It would only let the data to flow in computer which thus recognised and verified by one's system. Thus it only permits access to the system to ones already registered with the computer.

Digital Signature
Digital Signature created by using means of cryptography by applying algorithms. This has its prominent use in the business of banking where customer's signature thus identified by using this method.

Other Preventive Measures For Cyber Crimes
Prevention is always better than cure. A netizen should take certain precautions while operating the internet and should follow certain preventive measures which can defined as:

Identification of exposures through education will assist responsible companies and firms to meet these challenges.
One should avoid disclosing any personal information to strangers via e-mail or while chatting.

One must avoid sending any photograph to strangers by online as misusing of photograph incidents increasing day by day.

An update Anti-virus software to guard against virus attacks should used by all the netizens and should also keep back up volumes so that one may not suffer data loss in case of virus contamination.

A person should never send his credit card number to any site that however not secured, to guard against frauds.

Parents should keep a watch on sites that their children are accessing, to prevent any kind of harassment or deprivation in children.

Web site owners should watch traffic and check any irregularity on the site. It is the responsibility of the web site owners to adopt some policy for preventing cyber crimes as number of internet users are growing day by day.

Web servers running public sites must physically separately protected from internal corporate network.

It is better to use a security programmes by the body corporate to control information on sites.

Strict statutory laws need to passed by the Legislatures keeping in mind the interest of netizens.

IT department should pass certain guidelines and notifications for the protection of computer system and should also bring out with some more strict laws to breakdown the criminal activities relating to cyberspace.

As Cyber Crime thus the major threat to all the countries worldwide, certain steps should however taken at the international level for preventing the cyber crimes.

A complete justice must provided to the victims of cyber crimes by way of compensatory remedy and offenders to punish with highest type of punishment so that it will anticipate the criminals of cyber crime.

Preventive measures by Corporates
The first line of defence to prevent online consumers from becoming online victims is good education. Tips on the major forms of Internet fraud and how to combat them have been developed by public authorities, enforcement agencies, and the private sector on various platforms such as government websites, brochures, posters, videos, reports, etc. The International Consumer Protection and Enforcement Network (ICPEN), an informal network of enforcement authorities from OECD and other countries, has launched Fraud Prevention Month, an awareness campaign taking place on a designated month every year.

The private sector also offers a number of technical tools to provide consumers with real-time protection against cyber fraud. For example, business has developed means to counter spam messages, which are a significant source of fraud, through authentication, filters, and listings. Likewise, anti-phishing systems have been put in place allowing Internet users to report phishing sites and block them.

Preventive measures to be taken by corporates to protect their businesses –
Setup an e-security program for your business.

Ensure your security program facilitates confidentiality, integrity and availability.

Identify the sources of threats to your data from both internal and external sources. Examples: disgruntled employees - leaving bugs behind in your system, hackers looking to steal confidential information.

The security program that you create for your business must have provisions to maintenance and upgrades of your systems.

Administrators have access to all files and data. Therefore, one must be mindful of who is guarding the guards.

Roles for security should be defined, documented, and implemented for both your company and external contractors.

Establish a security awareness program for all users. Content should be communicated in non-technical terms. This could include briefings, posters, clauses in employee contracts, security awareness days etc.

Implement security training for technical staff that is focused on the security controls for their particular technical areas.

Maintain logs of all possible activities that may occur on your system. System records must note who was using the system, when, for how long, deletions etc.

User accounts should not be shared. User authorization should be mandatory. Employees should only be able to see information that they are authorized to see.

Employee user accounts must be disabled or removed when no longer needed. Example: in case an employee leaves the company.

Ensure network security from external sources by installing firewalls and intrusion detection systems.

Allow remote access to employees only through secure communication channels like SSL or VPN.

Install antivirus software on all desktops and servers. Buy Anti-Virus software solutions that allow real time upgrading of systems with anti-virus patches.

Create a data backup and disaster recovery plan in case of unforeseen natural calamities.

Ensure back-up procedures are in place and tested.

Ensure back-up procedures include all the critical as well as back office data such as finance, payroll etc.

Incident response is the ability to identify, evaluate, raise and address negative computer related security events.

In case of an incident, do not panic, and continue to save logs.

Incident response - Take a backup of the affected system and notify the authorities.

The draft National Cyber Security Policy of India has been prepared by CERT-In. The policy is intended to cater to a broad spectrum of ICT users and providers including

Government and non-Government entities. Besides this CERT-In in coordination with MHA, NIC and other stakeholders prepared and circulated Computer security guidelines and procedures for implementation across all Central Government Ministries/Departments.

7

REGULATORY AUTHORITIES In India

1) Department of Electronics and Information Technology

The functions of the Department of Electronics and Information Technology, Ministry of Communications & Information Technology, Government of India are as follows –

Policy matters relating to Information Technology, Electronics and Internet.

Initiatives for development of Hardware / Software industry including knowledge based enterprises, measures for promoting Information Technology exports and competitiveness of the industry.

Promotion of Information Technology and Information Technology enabled services and Internet.

Assistance to other departments in the promotion of E-Governance, E-Infrastructure, E-Medicine, E-Commerce, etc.

Promotion of Information Technology education and Information Technology-based education.

Matters relating to Cyber Laws, administration of the Information Technology Act. 2000 (21 of 2000) and other Information Technology related laws.

Matters relating to promotion and manufacturing of Semiconductor Devices in the country.

Interaction in Information Technology related matters with International agencies and bodies.

Initiative on bridging the Digital Divide, Matters relating to Media Lab Asia.

Promotion of Standardization, Testing and Quality in Information Technology and standardization of procedure for Information Technology application and Tasks.

Electronics Export and Computer Software Promotion Council (ESC).

National Informatics Centre (NIC)

All matters relating to personnel under the control of the Department.

2) Controller of Certifying Authorities (CCA)

The IT Act provides for the Controller of Certifying Authorities (CCA) to license and regulate the working of Certifying Authorities. The Certifying Authorities (CAs) issue digital signature certificates for electronic authentication of users.

The CCA certifies the public keys of CAs using its own private key, which enables users in the cyberspace to verify that a given certificate is issued by a licensed CA. For this purpose it operates, the Root Certifying Authority of India (RCAI).

3) Cyber Appellate Tribunal

Cyber Appellate Tribunal has been established under the IT Act under the aegis of Controller of Certifying Authorities (CCA). A Cyber Appellate Tribunal consists of one Presiding Officer who is qualified to be a Judge of a High Court or is or has been a member of the Indian Legal Service and is holding or has held a post in Grade I of that service for at least three years supported by other official under him/her.

The Cyber Appellate Tribunal has, for the purposes of discharging its functions under the IT Act, the same powers as are vested in a civil court under the Code of Civil Procedure, 1908. However, is not bound by the procedure laid down by the Code of Civil Procedure, 1908 but is guided by the principles of natural justice and, subject to the other provisions of this Act and of any rules. The Cyber Appellate Tribunal has powers to regulate its own procedure including the place at which it has its sittings.

Every proceeding before the Cyber Appellate Tribunal shall be deemed to be a judicial proceeding within the meaning of sections 193 and 228, and for the purposes of section 196 of the Indian Penal Code and the Cyber Appellate Tribunal shall be deemed to be a civil court for the purposes of section 195 and Chapter XXVI of the Code of Criminal Procedure, 1973.

The composition of the Cyber Appellate Tribunal is provided for under section 49 of the Information Technology Act, 2000. Initially the Tribunal consisted of only one person who was referred to as the Presiding Officer who was to be appointed by way of notification by the Central Government. Thereafter the Act was amended in the year 2008 by which section 49 which provides for the composition of the Cyber Appellate Tribunal has been changed. As per the amended section the Tribunal shall consist of a Chairperson and such number of other Members as the Central Government may by notification in the Official Gazette appoint. The selection of the Chairperson and Members of the Tribunal is made by the Central Government in consultation with the Chief Justice of India. The Presiding Officer of the Tribunal is now known as the Chairperson.

4) Indian Computer Emergency Response Team (ICERT)

The mission of ICERT is to enhance the security of India's Communications and Information Infrastructure through proactive action and effective collaboration. Its constituency is the Indian Cyber-community.

The purpose of the ICERT is, to become the nation's most trusted referral agency of the Indian Community for responding to computer security incidents as and when they occur; the ICERT will also assist members of the Indian Community in implementing proactive measures to reduce the risks of computer security incidents. It provides technical advice to system administrators and users to respond to computer security incidents. It also identifies trends in intruder activity, works with other similar institutions and organisations to resolve major security issues and disseminates information to the Indian cyber community.

It functions under the Department of Information Technology, Ministry of Communications & Information Technology, Government of India.

CLOUD COMPUTING

Cloud computing is internet based computing where virtual shared servers provide software, infrastructure, platform, devices and other resources and hosting to customers on a pay-as-you—use basis. All information that a digitized system has to offer is provided as a service in the cloud computing model. Users can access these services available on the "internet cloud" without having any previous know-how on managing the resources involved.

Thus, users can concentrate more on their core business processes rather than spending time and gaining knowledge on resources needed to manage their business processes.

Cloud computing customers do not own the physical infrastructure; rather they rent the usage from a third-party provider. This helps them to avoid huge expenses. They consume resources as a service and pay only for resources that they use. Most cloud computing infrastructures consist of services delivered through common centres and built on servers.

There are different types of clouds that one can subscribe depending on their needs –

Public Cloud - A public cloud can be accessed by any subscriber with an internet connection and access to the cloud space.

Private Cloud - A private cloud is established for a specific group or organization and limits access to just that group.

Community Cloud - A community cloud is shared among two or more organizations that have similar cloud requirements.

Hybrid Cloud - A hybrid cloud is essentially a combination of at least two clouds, where the clouds included are a mixture of public, private, or community.

The benefits of cloud computing for an enterprise include –

Reduction in upfront capital expenditure on hardware and software development. Consumption is usually billed on a utility (like phone bills) or subscription (like magazines) model. Users can terminate the contract at any time and are often covered by Service Level Agreements with financial penalties. This reduces risk and uncertainty and ensures them return on investment.
Location independence, as long as there is access to the internet.
Allows the enterprise to focus on its core business.
Increased competitive advantage.

Increased security at a much lesser cost as compared to traditional applications due to centralization of data and increased security focused resources.

Easy to maintain as they don't have to be installed on each user's computer.

Some of the other emerging trends apart from cloud computing of cyber law are listed below –

- Stringent regulatory rules are put in place by many countries to prevent unauthorized access to networks. Such acts are declared as penal offences.
- Stakeholders of the mobile companies will call upon the governments of the world to reinforce cyber-legal systems and administrations to regulate the emerging mobile threats and crimes.
- The growing awareness on privacy is another upcoming trend. Google's chief internet expert Vint Cerf has stated that *privacy may actually be an anomaly.*
- The growth of **Bitcoins** and other virtual currency is yet another trend to watch out for. Bitcoin crimes are likely to multiply in the near future.
- The arrival and acceptance of data analytics, which is another major trend to be followed, requires that appropriate attention is given to issues concerning **Big Data**.

CASE STUDIES of India(IT LAWS)

Cyber Crime's scenario in India(A Few Case study)

a) The Bank NSP Case

In this case a management trainee of a bank got engaged to a marriage. The couple used to exchange many emails using the company's computers. After some time they had broken up their marriage and the young lady created some fake email ids such as "Indian bar associations" and sent mails to the boy's foreign clients. She used the banks computer to do this. The boy's company lost a huge number of clients and took the bank to court. The bank was held liable for the emails sent using the bank's system.

b) Bazee.com case

In December 2004 the Chief Executive Officer of Bazee.com was arrested because he was selling a compact disk (CD) with offensive material on the website, and even CD was also conjointly sold- out in the market of Delhi. The Delhi police and therefore the Mumbai Police got into action and later the CEO was free on bail.

c) Parliament Attack Case

The Bureau of Police Research and Development, Hyderabad had handled this case. A laptop was recovered from the terrorist who attacked the Parliament. The laptop which was detained from the two terrorists, who were gunned down on 13 th December 2001 when the Parliament was under siege, was sent to Computer Forensics Division of BPRD. The laptop contained several proofs that affirmed the two terrorist's motives, mainly the sticker of the Ministry of Home that they had created on the laptop and affixed on their ambassador car to achieve entry into Parliament House and the fake ID card that one of the two terrorists was carrying with a Government of India emblem and seal. The emblems (of the 3 lions) were carefully scanned and additionally the seal was also craftly created together with a residential address of Jammu and Kashmir. However careful detection proved that it was all forged and made on the laptop.

d) Andhra Pradesh Tax Case

The owner of the plastics firm in Andhra Pradesh was arrested and cash of Rs. 22 was recovered from his house by the Vigilance Department. They wanted evidence from him concerning the unaccounted cash. The suspected person submitted 6,000 vouchers to prove the legitimacy of trade, however when careful scrutiny the vouchers and contents of his computers it unconcealed that every one of them were made after the raids were conducted. It had been concealed that the suspect was running 5 businesses beneath the presence of 1 company and used fake and computerized vouchers to show sales records and save tax. So the dubious techniques of the businessman from the state were exposed when officials of the department got hold of computers utilized by the suspected person.

e) SONY.SAMBANDH.COM CASE

India saw its 1st cybercrime conviction. This is the case where Sony India Private Limited filed a complaint that runs a website referred to as www.sony-sambandh.com targeting the NRIs. The website allows NRIs to send Sony products to their friends and relatives in India after they pay for it online. The company undertakes to deliver the products to the involved recipients. In May 2002, somebody logged onto the web site underneath the identity of Barbara Campa and ordered a Sony colour television set and a cordless head phone. She requested to deliver the product to Arif Azim in Noida and gave the number of her credit card for payment. The payment was accordingly cleared by the credit card agency and the transaction processed. After the related procedures of dues diligence and checking, the items were delivered to Arif Azim by the company. When the product was delivered, the company took digital pictures so as to indicate the delivery being accepted by Arif Azim. The transaction closed at that, but after one and a half months the credit card agency informed the company that this was an unauthorized transaction as the real owner had denied having made the purchase. The company had filed a complaint for online cheating at the CBI that registered a case under the Section 418, Section 419 and Section 420 of the IPC (Indian Penal Code). Arif Azim was arrested after the matter was investigated. Investigations discovered that Arif Azim, whereas acting at a call centre in Noida did gain access to the number of the credit card of an American national which he misused on the company's site. The CBI recovered the color television along with the cordless head phone. In this matter, the CBI had proof to prove their case so the accused admitted his guilt. The court had convicted Arif Azim under the Section 418, Section 419 and Section 420 of the IPC, this being the first time that a cybercrime has been convicted. The court, felt that since the defendant was a boy of 24 years and a first-time convict, a compassionate view needed to be taken. Thus, the court discharged the defendant on the probation for one year.

g) State of Tamil Nadu Vs Suhas Katti

The Case of Suhas Katti is notable for the fact that the conviction was achieved successfully within a relatively quick time of 7 months from the filing of the FIR. Considering that similar cases have been pending in other states for a much longer time, the efficient handling of the case which happened to be the first case of the Chennai Cyber Crime Cell going to trial deserves a special mention.

The case related to posting of obscene, defamatory and annoying message about a divorcee woman in the yahoo message group. E-Mails were also forwarded to the victim for information by the accused through a false e-mail account opened by him in the name of the victim. The posting of the message resulted in annoying phone calls to the lady in the belief that she was soliciting.

Based on a complaint made by the victim in February 2004, the Police traced the accused to Mumbai and arrested him within the next few days. The accused was a known family friend of the victim and was reportedly interested in marrying her. She however married another person. This marriage later ended in divorce and the accused started contacting her once again. On her reluctance to marry him, the accused took up the harassment through the Internet.

On 24-3-2004 Charge Sheet was filed u/s 67 of IT Act 2000, 469 and 509 IPC before The Hon'ble Addl. CMM Egmore by citing 18 witnesses and 34 documents and material objects. The same was taken on file in

C.C.NO.4680/2004. On the prosecution side 12 witnesses were examined and entire documents were marked as Exhibits.

The Defence argued that the offending mails would have been given either by ex-husband of the complainant or the complainant herself to implicate the accused as accused alleged to have turned down the request of the complainant to marry her. Further the Defence counsel argued that some of the documentary evidence was not sustainable under Section 65B of the Indian Evidence Act. However, the court relied upon the expert witnesses and other evidence produced before it, including the witnesses of the Cyber Cafe owners and came to the conclusion that the crime was conclusively proved.

Ld. Additional Chief Metropolitan Magistrate, Egmore, delivered the judgement on 5-11-04 as follows: " The accused is found guilty of offences under section 469, 509 IPC and 67 of IT Act 2000 and the accused is convicted and is sentenced for the offence to undergo RI for 2 years under 469 IPC and to pay fine of Rs.500/-and for the offence u/s 509 IPC sentenced to undergo 1 year Simple imprisonment and to pay fine of Rs.500/- and for the offence u/s 67 of

IT Act 2000 to undergo RI for 2 years and to pay fine of Rs.4000/- All sentences to run concurrently."
This is considered as the first case convicted under Section 67 of Information Technology Act 2000 in India.

h) Syed Asifuddin and Ors. V. The State of AP. & Anr., 2005CriLJ4314
Tata Indicom employees were arrested for manipulation of the electronic 32-bit number (ESN) programmed into cell phones that were exclusively franchised to Reliance Infocomm.

The court held that such manipulation amounted to tampering with computer source code as envisaged by section 65 of the Information Technology Act, 2000.

Reliance Infocomm launched a scheme under which a cell phone subscriber was given a digital handset worth Rs. 10,500/- as well as service bundle for 3 years with an initial payment of Rs. 3350/- and monthly outflow of Rs. 600/-. The subscriber was also provided a 1 year warranty and 3 year insurance on the handset. The condition was that the handset was technologically locked so that it would only work with the Reliance Infocomm services. If the customer wanted to leave Reliance services, he would have to pay some charges including the true price of the handset. Since the handset was of a high quality, the market response to the scheme was phenomenal.

Unidentified persons contacted Reliance customers with an offer to change to a lower priced Tata Indicom scheme. As part of the deal, their phone would be technologically "unlocked" so that the exclusive Reliance handsets could be used for the Tata Indicom service.

Reliance officials came to know about this "unlocking" by Tata employees and lodged a First Information Report (FIR) under various provisions of the Indian

Penal Code, Information Technology Act and the Copyright Act. The police then raided some offices of Tata Indicom in Andhra Pradesh and arrested a few Tata Tele Services Limited officials for reprogramming the Reliance handsets. These arrested persons approached the High Court requesting the court to quash the FIR on the grounds that their acts did not violate the said legal provisions.

Some of the issues raised by the defence in the case were - It is always open for the subscriber to change from one service provider to the other service provider; The subscriber who wants to change from Tata Indicom always takes his handset, to other service providers to get service connected and to give up Tata services; The handsets brought to Tata by Reliance subscribers are capable of accommodating two separate lines and can be activated on principal assignment mobile (NAM 1 or NAM 2). The mere activation of NAM 1 or NAM 2 by Tata in relation to a handset brought to it by a Reliance subscriber does not amount to any crime; A telephone handset is neither a computer nor a computer system containing a computer programmed; there is no law in force which requires the maintenance of "computer source code". Hence section 65 of the Information Technology Act does not apply.

Following were the observations of the Court –
- As per section 2 of the Information Technology Act, any electronic, magnetic or optical device used for storage of information received through satellite, microwave or other communication media and the devices which are programmable and capable of retrieving any information by manipulations of electronic, magnetic or optical impulses is a computer which can be used as computer system in a computer network.

- The instructions or programmed given to computer in a language known to the computer are not seen by the users of the computer/consumers of computer functions. This is known as source code in computer parlance.

- ESN and SID come within the definition of "computer source code" under section 65 of the Information Technology Act.

- When ESN is altered, the offence under Section 65 of Information Technology Act is attracted because every service provider has to maintain its own SID code and also give a customer specific number to each instrument used to avail the services provided.

i) P.R. Transport Agency Vs. Union of India (UOI)
Bharat Coking Coal Ltd (BCC) held an e-auction for coal in different lots. P.R. Transport

Agency's (PRTA) bid was accepted for 4000 metric tons of coal from Dobari Colliery. The acceptance letter was issued on 19th July 2005 by e-mail to PRTA's e-mail address. Acting upon this acceptance, PRTA deposited the full amount of Rs. 81.12 lakh through a cheque in favour of BCC. This cheque was accepted and encashed by BCC. BCC did not deliver the coal to PRTA. Instead it e-mailed PRTA saying that the sale as well as the e-auction in favour of PRTA stood cancelled "due to some technical and unavoidable reasons". The only reason for this cancellation was that there was some other person whose bid for the same coal was slightly higher than that of PRTA. Due to some flaw in the computer or it's programmed or feeding of data the higher bid had not been considered earlier. This communication was challenged by PRTA in the High Court of Allahabad.

BCC objected to the "territorial jurisdiction" of the Court on the grounds that no part of the cause of action had arisen within U.P. The communication of the acceptance of the tender was received by the petitioner by e-mail at Chandauli
(U.P.). Hence the contract (from which the dispute arose) was completed at Chandauli (U.P). The completion of the contract is a part of the "cause of action'. The place where the contract was completed by receipt of communication of acceptance is a place where 'part of cause of action' arises.

The Court observed –

- In reference to contracts made by telephone, telex or fax, the contract is complete when and where the acceptance is received. However, this principle can apply only where the transmitting terminal and the receiving terminal are at fixed points.

- In case of e-mail, the data (in this case acceptance) can be transmitted from anywhere by the e-mail account holder. It goes to the memory of a 'server' which may be located anywhere and can be retrieved by the addressee account holder from anywhere in the world. Therefore, there is no fixed point either of transmission or of receipt.

- Section 13(3) of the Information Technology Act has covered this difficulty of "no fixed point either of transmission or of receipt". According to this section "...an electronic record is deemed to be received at the place where the addressee has his place of business."

- The acceptance of the tender will be deemed to be received by PRTA at the places where it has place of business. In this case it is Varanasi and Chandauli (both in U.P.)

- The acceptance was received by PRTA at Chandauli / Varanasi. The contract became complete by receipt of such acceptance.

- Both these places are within the territorial jurisdiction of the High Court of Allahabad. Therefore, a part of the cause of action has arisen in U.P. and the court has territorial jurisdiction.

j) Ritu Kohli case

One Mrs. Ritu Kohli complained to the police against the a person who was using her identity to chat over the Internet at the website www.mirc.com, mostly in the Delhi channel for four consecutive days. Mrs. Kohli further complained that the person was chatting on the Net, using her name and giving her address and was talking obscene language. The same person was also deliberately giving her telephone number to other chatters encouraging them to call Ritu Kohli at odd hours. Consequently, Mrs Kohli received almost 40 calls in three days mostly at odd hours from as far away as Kuwait, Cochin, Bombay and Ahmedabad. The said calls created havoc in the personal life and mental peace of Ritu Kohli who decided to report the matter.

The IP addresses were traced and the police investigated the entire matter and ultimately arrested Manish Kathuria on the said complaint. Manish apparently pleaded guilty and was arrested. A case was registered under section 509, of the Indian Penal Code (IPC).

k) Avnish Bajaj Vs. State (N.C.T.) of Delhi

Avnish Bajaj – CEO of Baazee.com, a customer-to-customer website, which facilitates the online sale of property. Baazee.com receives commission from such sales and also generates revenue from advertisements carried on its web pages. An obscene MMS clipping was listed for sale on Baazee.com on 27th November, 2004 in the name of "DPS Girl having fun". Some copies of the clipping were sold through Baazee.com and the seller received the money for the sale. Avnish Bajaj was arrested under section 67 of the Information Technology Act, 2000.

The arguments of the defendant were that - Section 67 of the Information Technology Act relates to publication of obscene material. It does not relate to transmission of such material. On coming to learn of the illegal character of the sale, remedial steps were taken within 38 hours, since the intervening period was a weekend.

The findings of the Court –

It has not been established from the evidence that any publication took place by the accused, directly or indirectly.

The actual obscene recording/clip could not be viewed on the portal of Baazee.com.

The sale consideration was not routed through the accused.

Prima facie Baazee.com had endeavored to plug the loophole.

The accused had actively participated in the investigations.

The nature of the alleged offence is such that the evidence has already crystallized and may even be tamper proof.

Even though the accused is a foreign citizen, he is of Indian origin with family roots in India.

The evidence that has been collected indicates only that the obscene material may have been unwittingly offered for sale on the website.

The evidence that has been collected indicates that the heinous nature of

the alleged crime may be attributable to some other person.

The court granted bail to Mr. Bajaj subject to furnishing two sureties of Rs. 1 lakh each. The court ordered Mr. Bajaj to surrender his passport and not to leave India without the permission of the Court. The court also ordered Mr. /Bajaj to participate and assist in the investigation.

Why 2015 Was A Landmark Year For Indian Cyberlaw

The year 2015 was nothing if not eventful, and while some developments generated plenty of sound and fury, others made a quieter impact. As I look back at legal developments, what stands out is how 2015 was a landmark year in the evolution of cyberlaw in India.

This was the year in which the Supreme Court delivered its landmark judgment in the case of Shreya Singhal vs. Union of India. The apex court had been called upon to examine the constitutional validity of Section 66A of the Information Technology Act, 2000 and its various parameters from the perspective of the various principles enshrined in the Indian Constitution. In an unprecedented judgement it declared that the said section was unconstitutional, marking the day as a time of jubilation for free speech activists. However, the said judgment was also a landmark as it upheld the power of interception under Section 69A of the Information Technology Act, 2000 as enshrined under the law. The Supreme Court also upheld Section 79 of the Act, pertaining to intermediary liability, but with a caveat: intermediaries in India will have to act only on court order or on order of governmental agency. The said judgment once again reiterated the principle that any provision of law, concerning the real as well as virtual world, will have to ensure compliance with the Indian Constitution.

This was the year in which the Supreme Court delivered its landmark judgment in the case of Shreya Singhal vs. Union of India.

Given how the data economy is moving and the manner in which India is adopting the mobile ecosystem and the mobile web, it is only a question of time before the principles pertaining to intermediary liability will have to be relooked and reworked. Data repositories like intermediaries have to be made more accountable for third party data and information in their power and possession. It needs to be appreciated that the law must not be a tool in the hands of intermediaries to deny requests for legitimate access to information by users.

Later in the year, the government also introduced the draft National Encryption Policy for public comments. The policy was actually worded in very vague and broad terms so as to include within itself the requirement for every person to save all messages sent using encryption through all computer resources and mobile applications, including WhatsApp. The introduction of the said draft policy created a huge uproar, following which it was withdrawn. It was then announced that the policy would be reinitiated after taking into consideration all the concerns of the relevant stakeholders.

The year 2015 was also significant as it saw India hosting the International Conference on Cyberlaw, Cybercrime & Cybersecurity in New Delhi, with representatives of dozens of countries in attendance. The Hon'ble Chief Justice of India, Justice TS Thakur speaking at the conference emphasised the need for new laws to deal with cybercrimes and cyber terror. The conference deliberations and recommendations further contributed to the evolving cyberlaw jurisprudence in India.

The past year also saw the courts redefining, clarifying and dealing with the law pertaining to electronic evidence in India.

The past year also saw the courts redefining, clarifying and dealing with the law pertaining to electronic evidence in India. The courts in India followed the landmark case of Anvar PV vs. PK Basheer, wherein the Supreme Court clarified the law pertaining to electronic evidence. Indeed, this year saw the urgent need to simplify the rules of electronic evidence. Cyberlaw as a legal discipline needs to evolve in a user-friendly manner and the task of proving electronic records should not be an arduous exercise for the person relying upon the said electronic evidence.

Given the fact that a majority of Indians are today only using mobile devices to access the internet, it is high time that legal approaches to electronic evidence -- with specific reference to mobile evidence -- are reviewed and revised. The entire issue of production and proof of electronic evidence must be made less cumbersome for those wanting to rely on it.

Seen in totality, 2015 provided fertile grounds for further developments in cyber jurisprudence to take root and develop in the coming year.

IMPORTANT REFERENCES

http://deity.gov.in/ - Department of Electronics and Information Technology, Govt. of India
http://cybercellmumbai.gov.in/ - Cyber crime investigation cell http://ncrb.gov.in/ - National Crime Records Bureau http://catindia.gov.in/Default.aspx - Cyber Appellate Tribunal http://www.cert-in.org.in/ - Indian Computer Emergency Response Team http://cca.gov.in/rw/pages/index.en.do - Controller of Certifying Authorities
www.safescrypt.com - Safescrypt
www.nic.in – National Informatics Centre
www.idrbtca.org.in - IDRBT www.tcs-ca.tcs.co.in - TCS www.mtnltrustline.com - MTNL www.ncodesolutions.com - GNFC
www.e-Mudhra.com - e-Mudhra

Controller of Certifying Authorities
Electronics Niketan,
6 CGO Complex, Lodhi Road,
New Delhi – 110003
FAX : 91-011-24369578 info@cca.gov.in

Cyber Appellate Tribunal,
Ministry of Communications and Information Technology,
Department of Information Technology,
Jeevan Bharti (L.I.C.) Building, Ground Floor,
Outer Circle, Connaught Place,
New Delhi – 110001
Tel - 011-23355881

Indian Computer Emergency Response Team (CERT-In)
Department of Information Technology,
Ministry of Communications and Information Technology,
Government of India
Electronics Niketan,
6 CGO Complex, Lodhi Road,
New Delhi – 110003
Tel – 011-24368572

REFERENCES

[1] www.tigweb.org/action-tools/projects/download/4926.doc

[2]https://www.tutorialspoint.com/information_security_ cyber_law/introduction.htm

[3]https://www.slideshare.net/bharadwajchetan/an-introduction-to-cyber-law-it-act-2000-india

[4]http://www.academia.edu/7781826/IMPACT_OF_SOCI AL_MEDIA_ON_SOCIETY_and_CYBER_LAW

[5]https://cybercrime.org.za/definition

[6]http://vikaspedia.in/education/Digital%20Litercy/inf ormation-security/cyber-laws

[7]https://www.ijarcsse.com/docs/papers/Volume_3/5_ May2013/V3I5-0374.pdf

[8]http://searchsecurity.techtarget.com/definition/email-spoofing

[9]http://www.helplinelaw.com/employment-criminal-and-labour/CDII/cyber-defamation-in-india.html

[10] http://ccasociety.com/what-is-irc-crime/

[11] http://searchsecurity.techtarget.com/definition/denial-of-service

[12] http://niiconsulting.com/checkmate/2014/06/it-act-2000-penalties-offences-with-case-studies/

[13] http://www.cyberlawsindia.net/cyber-india.html

[14]https://en.wikipedia.org/wiki/Information_Technolo gy_Act,_2000

[15]https://www.ijarcsse.com/docs/papers/Volume_5/8_ August2015/V5I8-0156.pdf

[16]https://cybercrimelawyer.wordpress.com/category/i nformation-technology-act-section-65/

www.ingramcontent.com/pod-product-compliance
Lightning Source LLC
Chambersburg PA
CBHW051113050326
40690CB00006B/772